AF323696

TECHNIQUES
OF
ARTIFICIAL
INTELLIGENCE

STUART C. SHAPIRO
State University of New York at Buffalo

D. Van Nostrand Company
New York Cincinnati Toronto London Melbourne

D. Van Nostrand Company Regional Offices:
New York   Cincinnati

D. Van Nostrand Company International Offices:
London   Toronto   Melbourne

Copyright © 1979 by Litton Educational Publishing, Inc.

Library of Congress Catalog Card Number: 78-65449
ISBN: 0-442-80501-2

All rights reserved. No part of this work covered by the copyright hereon may be re-
produced or used in any form or by any means—graphic, electronic, or mechanical,
including photocopying, recording, taping, or information storage and retrieval systems—
without written permission of the publisher. Manufactured in the United States of
America.

Published by D. Van Nostrand Company
135 West 50th Street, New York, N. Y. 10020

10   9   8   7   6   5   4   3   2   1

Preface

This book consists of programming problems and examples of well-written programs in subareas of Artificial Intelligence (AI). The example programs are written in LISP, SNOBOL4, or MICROPLANNER, which are high-level languages available to and used by the AI community. Most of the programs are in LISP, which is by far the most commonly used language for AI research.

This book is not intended to be an introductory text, rather it is intended to supplement existing AI textbooks by presenting the details of the algorithms which they often discuss only in generalities. Each section contains a list of suggested collateral readings, well-documented and nicely stylized code, and suggested projects. It is expected that one of the texts listed in the suggested readings sections of the chapters (or a similar text) will be the main text of the course, and that the other texts and bibliography items will be available for reference in a library.

This book also is not intended to be an introduction to any programming language. It is expected that the reader will already have a basic knowledge of LISP, SNOBOL4, and MICROPLANNER by the time the relevant chapters are to be read. Of course, it is hoped that such basic knowledge will be greatly enhanced after studying the programs in this book and after doing the suggested projects.

It is my experience in teaching AI classes that students find the material very vague unless they are shown specific examples of programs that they can understand and run. I have also found it very successful to assign several 2–4 week programming problems in each 15 week semester, each problem drawn from a different subarea of AI and making use of the program examples from lecture. This book contains a set of these demonstration programs and suggested projects. The programming and documentation style used herein is intended to be a model for the students' projects.

I am grateful to my colleagues in the Computer Science Department of Indiana University for stimulating discussions on structured programming and LISP, notably Mitchell Wand, David Wise, and especially Daniel Friedman, whose obsession with LISP and style has done so much to mold the programming environment of the department. I am also grateful to the students who helped shape that environment, particularly Nick Eastridge, John Lowrance, John Martin, Don McKay, and Jim McKew. Computer services were provided by the IUPUI Computing Facilities as part of the I. U. Computing Network.

STUART C. SHAPIRO

Contents

Introduction   vii

1 Problem Solving   1
  1.1 Searching State Space Graphs   1
  1.2 Searching Problem—Reduction Graphs   10

2 Backtrack Programming   23
  2.1 The Eight Queens Problem   23
  2.2 The Missionary and Cannibal Problem   25

3 Game Playing   31
  3.1 Alpha-Beta Game Tree Searching   31
  3.2 A Program for a Specific Game: Kalah   35

4 Theorem Proving   57
  4.1 Wang's Algorithm   57
  4.2 The Resolution Method   62

5 Pattern Recognition and Vision   79
  5.1 Pattern Recognition   79
  5.2 Edge and Vertex Finding   85

6 Concept Formation 109

7 Deductive Question Answering 123

Appendix A Definitions of Some Useful Functions 141
A.1 REPEAT 141
A.2 DATA, NTH, and MAKENTH 142
A.3 PRIN3 143

Appendix B Functions Assumed to be Predefined 148
B.1 LISP Functions Assumed to be Predefined 148
B.2 MICROPLANNER Functions Assumed to be Predefined 156
B.3 SNOBOL4 Functions Assumed to be Predefined 157

Appendix C Index to Definitions of Functions 159

Bibliography 163

Introduction

Readings: Hunt, 1975–Chapter 1
                Jackson, 1974–Chapter 1
                Nilsson, 1971–Chapter 1
                Raphael, 1976–Chapter 1
                Winston, 1977–Chapter 1

LISP Texts: Allen, J., 1978
                Berkeley and Bobrow, 1964
                Friedman, 1974
                McCarthy et al., 1963
                Maurer, 1973
                Siklóssy, 1976
                Weissman, 1968

Each function used in this book is either defined in the section in which it is used, listed at the end of the section as a "problem specific function," defined in Appendix A as a generally useful function, or listed in Appendix B as a function assumed to be defined in the programming system. Appendix C is an index showing where each function is defined or otherwise listed.

There are two basic kinds of LISP functions used in this book. The more common is called an EXPR. It takes a fixed number of arguments evaluated before the function itself is evaluated. The less common is called a FEXPR. It takes an arbitrary number of arguments that are not evaluated before the function is called. The lambda variable of a FEXPR is bound to a list of the unevaluated arguments so that the function can do with them what it will. Check the manual of the LISP you will be using for the detailed differences.

The form of a LISP definition used below is

```
(DEFPROP function-name
   lambda-expression
EXPR-or-FEXPR)
```

and instead of writing (QUOTE S-expression), we write 'S-expression. Again, check your manual to see what you will be using.

A comment on EVAL versus EVALQUOTE: Some LISPs are "EVAL systems," some are "EVALQUOTE systems." It only makes a difference on the top level. Within function definitions, all systems use EVAL. If you don't know which your system is, try entering the following two lines:

```
(CONS (QUOTE A) (QUOTE (B))) NIL
CONS (A (B))
```

If the first line works and you get an error on the second, you have an EVAL system. If you get an error on the first line, but the second works, you have an EVALQUOTE system. This book assumes an EVAL system, but if you have an EVALQUOTE system, you should be able to adjust easily.

Many versions of LISP have been implemented on various computers and for various operating systems. Some functions have slightly different definitions in different systems, some take their arguments in different orders, and some are not provided in some implementations. This book uses Stanford LISP 1.6 as implemented on a DECsystem-10. A comparison of Appendix B.1 with your LISP manual will reveal the differences.

When a LISP function is defined in this book, the following are given:

1. A dummy call using the lambda variables for an EXPR, or variables in quotes for a FEXPR.

2. A comment explaining the function's arguments and the purpose of the function.

3. The definition of the function.

4. A comment on the way the code is written. This is usually omitted, since most of the code should be quite clear after minimal study.

In Sec. 5.1, we present material using SNOBOL4. There functions are defined in the following structured, modular fashion:

```
                    DEFINE ('Function ( . . . ) . . . ')
*
                    Comments describing the function, local variables, etc.
                    Assignment of pattern variables to be used in the function
                                                    : (Function_END)
Function            Body of Function
                    using Function.n for labels
Function_END
```

At this point, you should familiarize yourself with the system and the language you will use and with the functions given in Appendices A and B. Some of those functions have rather complicated definitions. It will be sufficient to understand what they may be used for.

Projects

1   If you will be using an interactive system, write a program that:

   1.   Greets the user in a friendly fashion.

   2.   Asks the user for his/her name.

   3.   If the user has been met previously, says something like, "Happy to see you again," otherwise says something like, "Pleased to meet you."

You will have to learn how to do I/O on your system, and how to read and write auxiliary files in order to save the list of previously seen names across runs of the program.

Chapter 1
Problem Solving

1.1 Searching State Space Graphs

Readings: Hart et al, 1968—pp. 100-107
Hunt, 1975—pp. 223-238
Jackson, 1974—pp. 80-87, 94-102
Nilsson, 1971—Chapters 2, 3
Raphael, 1976—pp. 55-86
Winston, 1977—Chapter 4

The following are the core functions for searching state space graphs. They will do depth-first, breadth-first, or uniform-cost search depending on how nodes are added to the open list. The basic design of the functions is the A* algorithm of Hart, Nilsson, and Raphael, 1968.

(SEARCH OPEN GOAL? OPS)

This is the main search loop. OPEN is a list of the start nodes. GOAL? is a predicate function that is True of a goal state. OPS is a list of operator functions that given a state return a list of successor states.

```
(DEFPROP SEARCH
  (LAMBDA (OPEN GOAL? OPS)
   (PROG   (NODE CLOSED)
           (RETURN
            (COND
             ((REPEAT
                WHILE OPEN
                     (SETQ NODE (CAR OPEN))
                     (SETQ OPEN  (CDR OPEN))
                     (SETQ CLOSED (CONS NODE CLOSED))
                UNTIL  (GOAL?  (STATE NODE))
```

```
                    (MAPC (FUNCTION ADD-TO-OPEN)
                          (EXPAND NODE OPS)))

            (LIST-SOLN NODE)
            '(IS THE SOLUTION))
           (T 'IMPOSSIBLE)))))
EXPR)
```

Note the basic search algorithm:

1. If the OPEN list is empty, there is no way to get from any start state to any goal state, so terminate, reporting failure.

2. Take the first node off the OPEN list and place it on the CLOSED list.

3. If it is a goal node, print the solution and terminate. Otherwise, expand it, getting a list of successors.

4. Put each successor node somewhere on the OPEN list. Sometimes this is not necessary for all successor nodes—see the function ADD-TO-OPEN.

5. Loop back to step (1).

To use the A* algorithm, we will use nodes containing the state of the problem, $\hat{g}$ of the node, $\hat{f}$ of the node, and the parent node of the node. We can use the DATA function to establish the data type and associated functions

```
(DATA NODE  (STATE GHAT FHAT PARENT))
```

where the uses of the fields are

STATE   a representation of the state of the problem

GHAT $\hat{g}$, the cost of the minimal cost path found so far from the root to this node

FHAT $\hat{f}$, an estimate of the cost of the minimal cost path from the root to a goal node through this node

PARENT   the parent node of this node, which is on the path measured by GHAT

```
(ADD-TO-OPEN NODE)
```

Adds the node NODE to the open list. If a node with the same state is already on either the open or closed list, the GHATs of the two nodes are compared. If the

GHAT of the new node is less than that of the old node, the old node is discarded and the new node is placed on OPEN. If the GHAT of the new node is equal to or greater than that of the old node, the new node is discarded.

```
(DEFPROP ADD-TO-OPEN
 (LAMBDA (NODE)
  (PROG (OLD)
        (COND
         ((SETQ OLD (ON? (STATE NODE) OPEN))
          (COND ((BETTER NODE OLD)
                 (SETQ OPEN (INSERTO NODE (REMOVE OLD OPEN))))
                (T NIL)))
         ((SETQ OLD (ON? (STATE NODE) CLOSED))
          (COND ((BETTER NODE OLD)(SETQ CLOSED (REMOVE OLD CLOSED))
                                  (SETQ OPEN (INSERTO NODE OPEN)))
                (T NIL)))
         (T (SETQ OPEN (INSERTO NODE OPEN))))))
EXPR)
```

If the "consistency condition"

$$\hat{h}(n) - \hat{h}(m) \leq k(n,m)$$

where $\hat{f}(n) = \hat{g}(n) + \hat{h}(n)$ and $k(n,m)$ is the cost of the minimal cost path from node n to node m, is satisfied and a node with the same state is found on CLOSED, the new node may be discarded without bothering with the BETTER check. The searches of both OPEN and CLOSED may be eliminated if the state space graph is a tree.

(EXPAND NODE OPS)

Returns a list of all successor nodes of NODE using the operators in the list OPS.

```
(DEFPROP EXPAND
 (LAMBDA (NODE OPS)
  (COND ((NULL OPS) NIL)
        (T (APPEND (MAKE ((CAR OPS) (STATE NODE)) NODE)
                   (EXPAND NODE (CDR OPS))))))
EXPR)
```

(MAKE STATE&COST PARENT)

STATE&COST is either NIL or a list whose first element is a successor state of the node PARENT and whose second element is the cost of getting to that state from

PARENT. If STATE&COST is NIL, NIL will be returned. Otherwise, a list will be returned whose only element is a node representing the new state.

```
(DEFPROP MAKE
 (LAMBDA (STATE&COST PARENT)
  (COND ((NULL STATE&COST) NIL)
        (T (LIST
             (NODE (CAR STATE&COST)
                   (PLUS (GHAT PARENT) (CADR STATE&COST))
                   (PLUS (GHAT PARENT)
                         (CADR STATE&COST)
                         (HHAT (CAR STATE&COST)))
                 PARENT)))))
EXPR)
```

If (HHAT (CAR STATE&COST)) is removed from the second sum, resulting in $\hat{f}(n) = \hat{g}(n)$, the uniform-cost algorithm will be implemented

---

```
(BETTER N M)
```

BETTER returns T if node N is better than node M, NIL otherwise.

```
(DEFPROP BETTER
 (LAMBDA (N M)
  (COND ((LESSP (FHAT N) (FHAT M)) T)
        ((LESSP (FHAT M) (FHAT N)) NIL)
        (T (GOAL? (STATE N)))))
EXPR)
```

```
(ON? STATE LIST)
```

If a node with state STATE is on the list LIST, the node is returned. Otherwise, NIL is returned.

```
(DEFPROP ON?
 (LAMBDA (STATE LIST)
  (COND
   ((REPEAT
      WHILE LIST
      UNTIL (EQUAL STATE (STATE (CAR LIST)))
           (SETQ LIST (CDR LIST)))
```

```
    (CAR LIST))
   (T NIL)))
EXPR)
```

```
(INSERTO NODE LIST)
```

Returns the list LIST with the node NODE inserted in order according to the function BETTER.

```
(DEFPROP INSERTO
 (LAMBDA  (NODE LIST)
  (COND  ((NULL LIST)  (LIST NODE))
         ((BETTER NODE (CAR LIST)) (CONS NODE LIST))
         (T  (CONS  (CAR LIST)  (INSERTO NODE  (CDR LIST))))))
EXPR)
```

If INSERTO were just defined as

```
        (LAMBDA  (NODE LIST)  (CONS NODE LIST))
```

depth-first searching would be done. If INSERTO were defined as

```
        (LAMBDA  (NODE LIST)  (SNOC LIST NODE))
```

breadth-first searching would be done.

```
(LIST-SOLN NODE)
```

Prints the states of the nodes on the path of PARENT links from NODE to NIL in reverse order. The first node printed will be a start node, the last will be NODE.

```
(DEFPROP LIST-SOLN
 (LAMBDA  (NODE)
  (COND  ((NULL NODE)  T)
         ((LIST-SOLN (PARENT NODE)) (PRINT (STATE NODE)))))
EXPR)
```

Problem-Specific Functions to be Added

```
(OPERATORi STATE)
```

A function representing each operator which is given a STATE and returns NIL if the operator does not apply, or a list whose first element is the successor state and whose second element is the cost of getting from STATE to the successor state via the operator.

(HHAT STATE)

Returns an estimate of the cost of getting to a goal state from the state STATE.

Leaving the functions as defined in this section, but defining HHAT to be always 0 will result in the uniform-cost algorithm. If in addition, the cost is always 1, breadth-first searching will be done.

(GOAL? STATE)

Returns T if STATE is a goal state, NIL otherwise.

Example

Having recently moved to Buffalo, New York, I was interested in the shortest route to my parent's home in Norwalk, Connecticut. Since it is not obvious from the map, let us use the state space program to decide. A useful function will be TRIP-SEG.

(TRIP-SEG CITY ROUTE)

Route is the representation of a route in the format
$$(C1\ D1,2\ C2 \ldots Dk\text{-}1,k\ Ck)$$
where Ci and $Ci+1$ are successive cities on the route and $Di, i+1$ is the distance from Ci to $Ci+1$ traveling on the route. If CITY is EQual to some $Cj\,(1 \leqslant j < k)$ on ROUTE, TRIP-SEG will return a list of the form $(Cj+1\ Dj, j+1)$. Otherwise, TRIP-SEG will return NIL.

```
(DEFPROP TRIP-SEG
 (LAMBDA (CITY ROUTE)
  (COND ((REPEAT
           WHILE (CDR ROUTE)
           UNTIL (EQ CITY (CAR ROUTE))
             (SETQ ROUTE (CDDR ROUTE)))
         (LIST (CADDR ROUTE) (CADR ROUTE)))
        (T NIL)))
EXPR)
```

Let us now define one operator for each major highway that looks possibly useful for getting from Buffalo to Norwalk,

```
(DEFPROP I90
 (LAMBDA (CITY)
  (TRIP-SEG CITY
```

```
                 '(BUFFALO 31 BATAVIA 28 WEST-HENRIETTA 80 SYRACUSE 134
                 ALBANY)))
EXPR)

(DEFPROP NY16
 (LAMBDA (CITY)
  (TRIP-SEG CITY  '(BUFFALO 70 HINSDALE)))
EXPR)

(DEFPROP NY17
 (LAMBDA (CITY)
  (TRIP-SEG CITY
             '(HINSDALE 61 AVOCA 100 BINGHAMTON 118 MIDDLETOWN 18
               HARRIMAN)))
EXPR)

(DEFPROP NY63
 (LAMBDA (CITY)
  (TRIP-SEG CITY  '(BATAVIA 54 DANSVILLE)))
EXPR)

(DEFPROP I390
 (LAMBDA (CITY)
  (TRIP-SEG CITY '(DANSVILLE 6 PERKINSVILLE 18 AVOCA)))
EXPR)

(DEFPROP US15
 (LAMBDA (CITY)
  (TRIP-SEG CITY  '(WEST-HENRIETTA 39 PERKINSVILLE)))
EXPR)

(DEFPROP I81
 (LAMBDA (CITY)
  (TRIP-SEG CITY '(SYRACUSE 81 BINGHAMTON)))
EXPR)

(DEFPROP I87
 (LAMBDA (CITY)
  (TRIP-SEG CITY '(ALBANY 88 NEWBURGH 15 HARRIMAN)))
EXPR)

(DEFPROP I84
 (LAMBDA (CITY)
  (TRIP-SEG CITY '(MIDDLETOWN 18 NEWBURGH 38 DANBURY)))
EXPR)

(DEFPROP I287
 (LAMBDA (CITY)
  (TRIP-SEG CITY '(HARRIMAN 45 PORT-CHESTER)))
EXPR)
```

```
(DEFPROP US7
 (LAMBDA (CITY)
  (TRIP-SEG CITY '(DANBURY 20 NORWALK)))
EXPR)
(DEFPROP I95
 (LAMBDA (CITY)
  (TRIP-SEG CITY '(PORT-CHESTER 16 NORWALK)))
EXPR)
```

and set OPS to be a list of the operators.

```
(SETQ OPS '(I90 NY16 NY17 NY63 I390 US15 I81 I87 I84 I287 US7 I95))
```

For $\hat{h}$, let us place on the property list of each city, its straight-line distance to Norwalk under the property DIST.

```
(MAPC (FUNCTION (LAMBDA (IV) (PUT (CAR IV) 'DIST (CADR IV))))
      '((BUFFALO 300) (BATAVIA 292) (HINSDALE 266) (WEST-HENRIETTA
        254) (DANSVILLE 242) (PERKINSVILLE 236) (AVOCA 222) (SYRACUSE
        194) (BINGHAMTON 148) (ALBANY 100) (MIDDLETOWN 56)
        (NEWBURGH 44) (HARRIMAN 40) (DANBURY 20)
        (PORT-CHESTER 16) (NORWALK 0)))
```

The function HHAT is then simple

```
(DEFPROP HHAT
 (LAMBDA (CITY) (GET CITY 'DIST))
EXPR)
```

We also need a goal function

```
(DEFPROP GOAL?
 (LAMBDA (CITY) (EQ CITY 'NORWALK))
EXPR)
```

and a start node

```
(SETQ START (NODE 'BUFFALO 0 300 NIL))
```

Finally, to get our problem solved, we enter,

```
(SEARCH (LIST START) (FUNCTION GOAL?) OPS)
```

and out comes

```
BUFFALO
BATAVIA
DANSVILLE
PERKINSVILLE
AVOCA
```

BINGHAMTON
MIDDLETOWN
NEWBURGH
DANBURY
NORWALK
(IS THE SOLUTION)

What do you know? That's what I thought!

Projects

1.1.1 Write a state space program to explore the "eight puzzle," which consists of
eight sliding blocks in a 3 by 3 tray as shown:

```
* * * * * * * * * * * *
*       *       *       *
*   1   *   2   *   3   *
*       *       *       *
* * * * * * * * * * * *
*       *       *       *
*   4   *   5   *   6   *
*       *       *       *
* * * * * * * * * * * *
*       *       * * * * *
*   7   *   8   * * * * *
*       *       * * * * *
* * * * * * * * * * * *
```

1.1.2 Write a state space program to explore the sliding block puzzle shown below:

```
* * * * * * * * * * * * * * * * * * * *
*       *     * * * * *       *       *
*       *     * * * * *       *       *
*       *     * * * * *       *       *
*   2   *   3 * * * * *   8   *   9   *
*       *     * * * * *       *       *
*       *     * * * * *       *       *
*       *     * * * * *       *       *
* * * * * * * * * * * * * * * * * * * *
*               *       *           *
*               *   5   *       7   *
*       1       *       *           *
*               * * * * * * * * * * * *
*               *       *           *
*               *   4   *       6   *
*               *       *           *
* * * * * * * * * * * * * * * * * * * *
```

1.1.3 Design a maze and write a state space program to solve it.

1.1.4 Write a state space program to solve any of the following class of water jug problems:

> There are two jugs, one holds $m1$ gallons, the other $m2$ gallons.
> You may pour the contents of one jug into the other until you either empty the former or fill the latter.
> You may dump the entire contents of either jug down the drain.
> You may fill either jug from a water tap. (In some problems, this is not allowed.)
> Starting with x gallons in one jug and y gallons in the other, wind up with z gallons in one of them.

1.1.5 Write a state space program to solve the Tower of Hanoi problem:

> There are three poles: A, B, and C
> There are n different size discs.
> At the start, the discs are on pole A, in order of size, the largest on the bottom.
> Transfer all the discs to pole C according to the following rules:
>> Move only one disc at a time.
>> Never put a disc on a smaller disc.

1.2 Searching Problem—Reduction Graphs

Readings: Chang and Slagle, 1971
Hunt, 1975—pp. 240-243
Jackson, 1974—pp. 88-93
Nilsson, 1971—pp. 80-137
Winston, 1977—Chapter 4

We will search problem-reduction graphs by reducing them to state space graphs, and using the search routines of Chapter 1.1. The state of a state space node will be a problem tree. After expanding a problem node into an AND/OR tree, we will transform the state space tree into a kind of disjunctive normal form, in which the successors of any branch node represent alternative ways of solving the problem represented by the branch node and each terminal node represents a set of problems, all of which must be solved to solve the original problem.

We will establish a data type called PNODE to represent a problem node. A PNODE will be the value of the STATE field of each state space NODE.

(DATA PNODE (STATE AVSO STATUS SUCCESSORS))

The fields of a PNODE are as follows

      STATE   a representation of the problem represented by the PNODE

AVSO	NIL if it's an And node
	T if it's an Or node
STATUS	T if the problem is solved
	NIL if it is unsolvable
	? if it is not yet known which
SUCCESSORS	the successor PNODEs

(AND-NODE N)

Returns T if the successors of the PNODE N must all be solved to solve the problem represented by N, NIL otherwise.

```
(DEFPROP AND-NODE
 (LAMBDA (N) (NOT (AVSO N)))
EXPR)
```

(OR-NODE N)

Returns T if any successor of the PNODE N represents an alternative way of solving the problem represented by N.

```
(DEFPROP OR-NODE
 (LAMBDA (N) (AVSO N))
EXPR)
```

(GOAL? PN)

Returns T if the PNODE PN (which is the STATE of some state space node) is a goal state of the state space graph, NIL otherwise. It is a goal if it represents a solved problem. This is one of the "problem-specific functions" listed in Sec. 1.1.

```
(DEFPROP GOAL?
 (LAMBDA (PN) (EQ (STATUS PN) T))
EXPR)
```

(EXPAND NODE OPS)

Returns a list of all successors of the state space node NODE using the problem reduction operators in the list OPS on the problems of NODE.

```
(DEFPROP EXPAND
 (LAMBDA  (NODE OPS)
  (MAKE* NODE (GET&NODES (EXPAND1 (SUCCESSORS (STATE NODE)) OPS))))
EXPR)
```

Since NODE is an unexpanded node, its STATE is an AND PNODE whose SUCCESSORS are PNODEs each representing a single problem.

This is a redefinition of the EXPAND of Sec. 1.1, required because in the Sec. 1.1 version the operators in OPS apply directly to the STATE of NODE, whereas here they apply to the STATEs of each PNODE in the list of SUCCESSORS of the STATE of NODE.

(MAKE* PARENT L&NODES)

Returns a list of successor state space nodes to the state space node PARENT. Each successor has as its STATE one of the AND PNODEs in the list L&NODES, except that unsolvable PNODEs have been discarded.

```
(DEFPROP MAKE*
 (LAMBDA  (PARENT L&NODES)
  (COND ((NULL L&NODES)  NIL)
        ((NULL (STATUS (CAR L&NODES))) (MAKE* PARENT (CDR L&NODES)))
        (T (CONS (MAKE (CAR L&NODES) PARENT)
                 (MAKE* PARENT (CDR L&NODES))))))
EXPR)
```

MAKE* and its help function MAKE replace the function MAKE of Sec. 1.1.

(MAKE &NODE PARENT)

Returns a state space NODE whose STATE is the AND PNODE, &NODE and whose PARENT is the NODE, PARENT.

```
(DEFPROP MAKE
 (LAMBDA (&NODE PARENT)
  (NODE &NODE
        (ADD1 (GHAT PARENT))
        (PLUS (ADD1 (GHAT PARENT)) (HHAT &NODE))
        PARENT))
EXPR)
```

```
(GET&NODES NODELIST)
```

NODELIST is a list of expanded PNODES, all of which must be solved to solve the original problem. GET&NODES returns a list of AND PNODES, which are alternative ways of solving the problem.

```
(DEFPROP GET&NODES
 (LAMBDA (NODELIST)
  (COND    ((NULL NODELIST) NIL)
           (T (SUCCESSORS (ASSOCIATE (DNF (BUILD NIL NIL NODELIST)))))))))
EXPR)
```

```
(EXPAND1 TNODES OPS)
```

TNODES is a list of terminal PNODEs. That is, each one is either solved or represents a single problem. EXPAND1 expands each unsolved PNODE using the operators on the list OPS and returns a list of the solved and expanded PNODEs.

```
(DEFPROP EXPAND1
 (LAMBDA (TNODES OPS)
  (COND    ((NULL TNODES) NIL)
           ((EQ (STATUS (CAR TNODES)) T)
            (CONS (CAR TNODES) (EXPAND1 (CDR TNODES) OPS)))
           (T (CONS (EXPAND2 (CAR TNODES) OPS)
                    (EXPAND1 (CDR TNODES) OPS)))))
EXPR)
```

```
(EXPAND2 TNODE OPS)
```

TNODE is a terminal PNODE, and OPS is a list of operators. EXPAND2 returns an OR PNODE, each of whose successors represents an alternative way of solving the problem represented by TNODE.

```
(DEFPROP EXPAND2
 (LAMBDA (TNODE OPS)
  (PROG    (L&NODES)
           (REPEAT
             WHILE OPS
                     (SETQ L&NODES
                       (APPEND
                         (MAKE&NODE ((CAR OPS) (STATE TNODE)))
                         L&NODES))
```

```
                    (SETQ OPS (CDR OPS)))
          (RETURN  (BUILD (STATE TNODE) T L&NODES)))))
EXPR)
```

```
(MAKE&NODE PROBLEMS)
```

If PROBLEMS is an empty list, it returns an empty list. Otherwise, it returns a list containing one AND PNODE whose successors are terminal PNODES, each representing one problem on the list, PROBLEMS.

```
(DEFPROP MAKE&NODE
 (LAMBDA (PROBLEMS)
   (COND   ((NULL PROBLEMS) NIL)
           (T (LIST
               (BUILD NIL NIL (MAPCAR (FUNCTION MAKETNODE)
               PROBLEMS))))))
EXPR)
```

```
(MAKETNODE PROBLEM)
```

Returns a terminal PNODE whose STATE is the problem, PROBLEM.

```
(DEFPROP MAKETNODE
 (LAMBDA (PROBLEM)
  (PNODE PROBLEM T (OR (PRIMITIVE PROBLEM) '? NIL))
EXPR)
```

```
(BUILD STATE OR? SUCCS)
```

Returns a PNODE whose STATE field is STATE, whose AVSO field is OR?, whose SUCCESSORS field is SUCCS, and whose STATUS field is determined by properly backing up the STATUS fields of its successors.

```
(DEFPROP BUILD
 (LAMBDA (STATE OR? SUCCS)
  (PNODE STATE OR? (BACKUP OR? SUCCS (NOT OR?)) SUCCS))
EXPR)
```

(BACKUP OR? LPNODES BSTAT)

If the STATUS of any PNODE on the list, LPNODES is OR?, OR? is returned. Otherwise if the STATUS of any of them is ?, ? is returned. Otherwise, BSTAT is returned.

```
(DEFPROP BACKUP
 (LAMBDA (OR? LPNODES BSTAT)
  (COND    ((NULL LPNODES) BSTAT)
           ((EQ (STATUS (CAR LPNODES)) OR?) OR?)
           ((EQ (STATUS (CAR LPNODES)) '?)
            (BACKUP OR? (CDR LPNODES) '?))
           (T (BACKUP OR? (CDR LPNODES) BSTAT))))
EXPR)
```

(DNF PN)

Returns a problem tree equivalent to the one whose root is PN, but in disjunctive normal form.

```
(DEFPROP DNF
 (LAMBDA (PN)
  (COND    ((TERMINAL? PN) PN)
           (T (DISTRIB&
               (SUCCESSORS PN (MAPCAR (FUNCTION DNF) (SUCCESSORS
                PN)))))))
EXPR)
```

(TERMINAL? PN)

Returns T if the PNODE, PN has no successors, NIL otherwise.

```
(DEFPROP TERMINAL?
 (LAMBDA (PN) (NULL (SUCCESSORS PN)))
EXPR)
```

(DISTRIB& N)

N is the root of a problem tree. If it is an AND node and has an OR successor, DISTRIB& uses the distributive law to return an equivalent tree whose root is an OR node.

```
(DEFPROP DISTRIB&
 (LAMBDA (N)
  (COND  ((AND-NODE N) (DISTRIB N (FIRST-OR (SUCCESSORS N)))) (T N)))
EXPR)
```

```
(FIRST-OR LN)
```

Returns the first nonterminal OR node on the list LN.

```
(DEFPROP FIRST-OR
 (LAMBDA (LN)
  (COND  ((NULL LN) NIL)
         ((TERMINAL? (CAR LN)) (FIRST-OR (CDR LN)))
         ((OR-NODE (CAR LN)) (CAR LN))
         (T (FIRST-OR (CDR LN)))))
EXPR)
```

```
(DISTRIB N& NV)
```

N& is an AND PNODE and NV is an OR PNODE, which is a successor of N&. DISTRIB removes NV from the successors of N& and distributes the modified N& across the successors of NV, returning the modified NV.

```
(DEFPROP DISTRIB
 (LAMBDA (N& NV)
  (COND  ((NULL NV) N&)
         (T (STATUS
             (DISTRIB1 NV
                       (SUCCESSORS N& (REMOVE NV (SUCCESSORS N&))))
             (MIN (STATUS NV) (STATUS N&))))))
EXPR)
```

```
(DISTRIB1 NV N&)
```

Distributes the AND PNODE N& across the successors of the OR PNODE NV, and applies the distributive law recursively. The modifed NV is returned.

```
(DEFPROP DISTRIB1
 (LAMBDA (NV N&)
  (SUCCESSORS NV
```

```
                    (MAPCAR (FUNCTION DISTRIB&)
                            (DISTRIB2 N& (SUCCESSORS NV)))))
EXPR)
```

```
(DISTRIB2 N& LN)
```

Returns a list of AND PNODEs, each of which is a copy of N& with a different member of the list of nodes, LN added as an additional successor. The STATUS of each AND NODE is adjusted appropriately.

```
(DEFPROP DISTRIB2
 (LAMBDA (N& LN)
   (COND   ((NULL LN) NIL)
           (T (CONS (STATUS (SUCCESSORS N&
                                        (CONS (CAR LN)
                                              (SUCCESSORS N&)))
                            (MIN-STAT (STATUS N&) (STATUS (CAR LN))))
                    (DISTRIB2 N & (CDR LN))))))
EXPR)
```

```
(MIN-STAT S1 S2)
```

Returns the minimum of the two STATUSes S1 and S2 according to the ordering $NIL < ? < T$.

```
(DEFPROP MIN-STAT
 (LAMBDA (S1 S2)
   (COND   ((EQ S1 T) S2)
           ((NULL S1) NIL)
           ((NULL S2) NIL)
           (T '?)))
EXPR)
```

```
(ASSOCIATE N)
```

Applies the associative law to the problem tree whose root is N, so that no PNODE has a successor with the same AVSO. The modified N is returned.

```
(DEFPROP ASSOCIATE
 (LAMBDA (N)
```

```
(ASSOCIATE1 (MAPCAR (FUNCTION ASSOCIATE) (SUCCESSORS N))
            (SUCCESSORS N NIL)))
EXPR)
```

```
(ASSOCIATE1 LN N)
```

N is a PNODE, and LN is the list of N's successors, all of which are in disjunctive normal form with the associative law fully applied. Any nonterminal node in LN with the same AVSO as N is eliminated, and its successors are made successors of N. Duplicate PNODEs are also eliminated from this new list of successors. The modified N is returned.

```
(DEFPROP ASSOCIATE1
 (LAMBDA (LN N)
  (PROG  (LNN)
         (REPEAT
          WHILE LN
               (COND ((TERMINAL? (CAR LN))
                      (SETQ LNN (INSERTPN (CAR LN) LNN)))
                     ((EQ (AVSO (CAR LN)) (AVSO N))
                      (SETQ LNN
                            (UNIONPN (SUCCESSORS (CAR LN)) LNN)))
                     (T (SETQ LNN (INSERTPN (CAR LN) LNN))))
               (SETQ LN (CDR LN)))
         (RETURN (SUCCESSORS N LNN))))
EXPR)
```

```
(INSERTPN S L)
```

The list of PNODEs, L is returned with the PNODE S added, unless a node equivalent to S is already on L, in which case L is returned unchanged.

```
(DEFPROP INSERTPN
 (LAMBDA (S L)
  (COND  ((NULL L) (LIST S))
         ((EQPNODE S (CAR L)) L)
         (T (CONS (CAR L) (INSERTPN S (CDR L))))))
EXPR)
```

```
(UNIONPN L1 L2)
```

The union of the two sets of PNODES, L1 and L2 is returned.

```
(DEFPROP UNIONPN
 (LAMBDA (L1 L2)
  (PROG2 (REPEAT
             WHILE L1
                   (SETQ L2 (INSERTPN (CAR L1) L2))
                   (SETQ L1 (CDR L1)))
            L2))
EXPR)
```

```
(EQPNODE PN1 PN2)
```

Returns T if PN1 and PN2 are equivalent PNODEs; NIL otherwise.

```
(DEFPROP EQPNODE
 (LAMBDA (PN1 PN2)
  (AND (EQUAL (STATE PN1) (STATE PN2))
       (EQ (AVSO PN1) (AVSO PN2))
       (EQ (STATUS PN1) (STATUS PN2))
       (EQSETS (SUCCESSORS PN1) (SUCCESSORS PN2))))
EXPR)
```

```
(EQSETS SPN1 SPN2)
```

Returns T if SPN1 and SPN2 are equivalent sets of PNODEs.

```
(DEFPROP EQSETS
 (LAMBDA (SPN1 SPN2)
  (COND   ((NULL SPN1) (NULL SPN2))
          ((NULL SPN2) NIL)
          ((SETQ SPN2 (ROTATE SPN2 (CAR SPN1)))
           (EQSETS (CDR SPN1) (CDR SPN2)))
          (T NIL)))
EXPR)
```

```
(ROTATE SPN PN)
```

If a PNODE equivalent to PN is on the list of PNODEs, SPN, then SPN is returned reordered so that that PNODE occurs first. Otherwise, NIL is returned.

```
(DEFPROP ROTATE
 (LAMBDA (SPN PN)
  (PROG (SPNF)
```

```
(RETURN (COND ((REPEAT
                   WHILE SPN
                   UNTIL (EQPNODE (CAR SPN) PN)
                       (SETQ SPNF (CONS (CAR SPN) SPNF))
                       (SETQ SPN (CDR SPN)))
                (APPEND SPN SPNF))
              (T NIL)))))
EXPR)
```

Problem-Specific Functions to be Added

(PRIMITIVE PROBLEM)

Returns T if PROBLEM represents a primitive problem, NIL otherwise.

(OP*i* PROBLEM)

A function representing each problem-reduction operator, which is given PROB-LEM, a representation of a problem, and returns a list of problem representations such that PROBLEM can be solved by solving all the problems on the list (OP*i* PROBLEM). If PROBLEM cannot be reduced by OP*i*, it should return NIL.

(HHAT &NODE)

Returns an estimate of the number of reduction steps necessary to reduce all the problems of (SUCCESSORS &NODE) to primitive problems.

Example

As a brief example, let us use the problem-solving method of this section to prove that two unordered binary trees (UB-Trees) are equivalent.

Let us define the LISP representation of a UB-Tree as either an atom or a list of two UB-Trees where the order of the two trees in the list is irrelevant.

The representation of a problem will be a list of two UB-Trees. The problem is to show them equivalent.

Two UB-Trees are equivalent if their LISP representations are EQUAL. We will use this to define what a primitive problem is.

```
(DEFPROP PRIMITIVE
 (LAMBDA (PROB)
  (EQUAL  (CAR PROB) (CADR PROB)))
EXPR)
```

If two UB-Trees are nonatomic, they are equivalent if the first UB-Trees of each list are equivalent and the second UB-Trees of each list are equivalent. This defines one problem reduction operator.

```
(DEFPROP OP1
  (LAMBDA (PROB)
   (COND  ((LESSP (LENGTH (CAR PROB)) 2) NIL)
          ((LESSP (LENGTH (CADR PROB)) 2) NIL)
          (T (LIST (LIST (CAAR PROB) (CAADR PROB))
                   (LIST (CADAR PROB) (CADADR PROB))))))
 EXPR)
```

Two nonatomic UB-Trees are equivalent if the first subtree of one representation is equivalent to the second of the other and vice versa. This defines another problem reduction operator.

```
(DEFPROP OP2
  (LAMBDA (PROB)
   (COND  ((LESSP (LENGTH (CAR PROB)) 2) NIL)
          ((LESSP (LENGTH (CADR PROB)) 2) NIL)
          (T (LIST (LIST (CAAR PROB) (CADADR PROB))
                   (LIST (CADAR PROB) (CAADR PROB))))))
 EXPR)
```

In any other case, the two UB-Trees are not equivalent. So our set of operators is just OP1 and OP2.

```
(SETQ OPS '(OP1 OP2))
```

Since each operator reduces the depth of the trees by one level and the depth of the tree is a reasonable measure of the expected cost of solving the equivalence problem, we may as well use a breadth-first search. We do this by making HHAT the constant zero function.

```
(DEFPROP HHAT
  (LAMBDA (&NODE) 0)
 EXPR)
```

For our example problem, let us prove the equivalence of the two trees ((A (B C)) (D (E F))) and (((E F) D) (A (C B))).

```
(SETQ PROBLEM '(((A (B C)) (D (E F)))
                (((E F) D) (A (C B)))))
```

A leaf problem node is always an AND-node whose SUCCESSORS are problem nodes whose STATES are unexpanded problems. So our initial problem node is as follows.

```
(SETQ INITIAL-P-NODE
      (PNODE NIL NIL ? (LIST (PNODE PROBLEM T ? NIL))))
```

Finally, we make a start node of a state space by making a NODE whose STATE is our initial PNODE.

```
(SETQ START (NODE INITIAL-P-NODE 0 0 NIL))
```

Now we are ready to get our problem solved by entering:

```
(SEARCH (LIST START) (FUNCTION GOAL?) OPS)
```

The answer (slightly edited for readability) is

```
(PNODE NIL NIL ? ((PNODE (((A (B C)) (D (E F)))
                          (((E F) D) (A (C B))))
                    T ? NIL)))
(PNODE NIL NIL ? ((PNODE ((A (B C)) (A (C B))) T ? NIL)
                  (PNODE ((D (E F)) ((E F) D)) T ? NIL)))
(PNODE NIL NIL ? ((PNODE (D D) T T NIL)
                  (PNODE ((E F) (E F)) T T NIL)
                  (PNODE (A A) T T NIL)
                  (PNODE ((B C) (C B)) T ? NIL)))
(PNODE NIL NIL T ((PNODE (B B) T T NIL)
                  (PNODE (C C) T T NIL)
                  (PNODE (D D) T T NIL)
                  (PNODE ((E F) (E F)) T T NIL)
                  (PNODE (A A) T T NIL)))
(IS THE SOLUTION)
```

which constitutes a proof that the two UB-Trees are equivalent.

It would be easier if we had the function

(SEARCH PROBLEM OPERATORS)

which is given a problem and a list of operators and calls SEARCH with the appropriate initial state space node. This is left as an exercise for the reader.

Projects

1.2.1 Write a problem reduction program to solve the Tower of Hanoi problem stated in project 1.1.5.

1.2.2 Write a problem reduction program to do symbolic integration. Find problem reduction operators and a list of primitive problems in a table of integrals such as in the Chemical Rubber Company's *Standard Mathematical Tables*.

1.2.3 Write a problem reduction program to prove theorems in plane geometry. A problem is a list of assumed propositions and a proposition to be proved. Problem-reduction operators are proof methods such as, "To show two triangles congruent, show that the three sides of one are equal to the corresponding sides of the other."

Chapter 2

Backtrack Programming

Readings: Sussman and Winograd, 1970
Nilsson, 1971–pp. 24-27, 90-93
Baumgart, 1972
Jackson, 1974–pp. 257-264
Hunt, 1975–pp. 281-286

MICROPLANNER is a language that does automatic backtracking and thus allows us to write state space search programs in a "nondeterministic" manner.

In the code in this chapter, MICROPLANNER variables are written $?X. In some implementations of the language, that would be written (THV X). (THEV S) is a form that forces the evaluation of S. We write it as $ES.

2.1 The Eight Queens Problem

The eight queens problem is a classic backtracking problem. The problem is to place eight queens on a chess board so that no queen is attacking any other. In other words, no two queens are to be on the same row, column, or diagonal. We adapt the approach of Wirth, 1971 to a MICROPLANNER state space approach.

The problem is to place eight queens. We associate the ith queen with the ith row. This eliminates the possibility of placing two queens on the same row. We use eight operators of the form, "place a queen on the jth column," and forbid an operator to be used twice on any potential solution branch. This eliminates the possibility of placing two queens on the same column. Finally, we keep track of the right and left diagonals being occupied, and do not allow another queen on an occupied diagonal.

We will use MICROPLANNER's data base to record the necessary information. The eight operators will be assertions of the form (CLM (j)) and will be THERASEd to make them unavailable. When queen i is placed on column j, we will THASSERT the assertions (RDIAG (i-j)) and (LDIAG (i+j)) to note that these two diagonals are in use.

We will drive the problem solver with the consequent theorem PLACE.

PLACE THCONSE (QUEEN $?R)

PLACE is a consequent theorem used to find places for the first $?R queens.

```
(THASSERT
 (DEFPROP PLACE
  (THCONSE (R C) (QUEEN $?R)
   (THGOAL (CLM $?C))
   (THERASE (CLM $?C))
   (THASSERT (RDIAG $E(RDIAG $?R $?C)))
   (THASSERT (LDIAG $E(LDIAG $?R $?C)))
   (THGOAL (QUEEN $E(LIST (SUB1 (CAR $?R))))) (THUSE PLACE))
   (PRIN3 PLACE QUEEN * $?R ON COLUMN *$?C <>))
THEOREM))
```

PLACE carries out the following operations:

1. Find an available operator (column) for the Rth queen.

2. Remove that operator from the collection of available operators.

3. Reserve the right diagonal.

4. Reserve the left diagonal.

5. Find places for the first $R - 1$ queens.

6. Print the column of the Rth queen.

Steps 1, 3, 4, and 5 might fail, in which case automatic backup would occur.

(RDIAG R C)

Returns the number of the lower left to upper right diagonal on which the square in the Rth row and Cth column is. Each of the three numbers is really a list of one number.

```
(DEFPROP RDIAG
 (LAMBDA (R C) (LIST (DIFFERENCE (CAR R) (CAR C))))
EXPR)
```

(LDIAG R C)

Returns the number of the lower right to upper left diagonal on which the square in the Rth row and Cth column is. Each of the three numbers is really a list of one number.

```
(DEFPROP LDIAG
 (LAMBDA (R C) (LIST (PLUS (CAR R) (CAR C))))
EXPR)
```

To execute the program, we first assert the eight operators:

```
(THASSERT (CLM (8)))
(THASSERT (CLM (7)))
(THASSERT (CLM (6)))
(THASSERT (CLM (5)))
(THASSERT (CLM (4)))
(THASSERT (CLM (3)))
(THASSERT (CLM (2)))
(THASSERT (CLM (1)))
```

Next, we assert that zero queens are in place.

```
(THASSERT (QUEEN (0)))
```

Finally, we ask if eight queens can be placed.

```
(THGOAL (QUEEN (8)) (THUSE PLACE))
```

The output is:

```
PLACE QUEEN (1) ON COLUMN (4)
PLACE QUEEN (2) ON COLUMN (2)
PLACE QUEEN (3) ON COLUMN (7)
PLACE QUEEN (4) ON COLUMN (3)
PLACE QUEEN (5) ON COLUMN (6)
PLACE QUEEN (6) ON COLUMN (8)
PLACE QUEEN (7) ON COLUMN (5)
PLACE QUEEN (8) ON COLUMN (1)
```

2.2 The Missionary and Cannibal Problem

The problem is that three missionaries and three cannibals are on the left bank of a river. None of them can swim, but they have a boat that holds at most two people, although it could be rowed by one person alone. The missionaries and cannibals all want to get across the river together, but if the cannibals ever outnumber the missionaries on either bank, their old habits will overcome them, and they will eat the missionaries. How can all six people get across the river safely?

We will do this as a state space search program in MICROPLANNER. To represent a state, we will use an assertion of the form (MC ($i\,j$) side), where side is either LEFT or RIGHT and the assertion represents the state in which there are i missionaries and *j* cannibals on the side-th bank of the river and the boat is also on the side-th bank. The start state will be (MC (3 3) LEFT), and the goal state will be (MC (3 3) RIGHT). The operators will be boat crews. Note that each operator is symmetric—if an operator will take state *si* into state *sj*, it will also take state *sj* into state *si*. We will rely on this symmetry in our program.

We will use the global MAX to hold the maximum number of people of each group.

(SETQ MAX 3)

CROSS THCONSE (MC $?MC $?B)

CROSS is a consequent theorem that finds a way to get (CAR $?MC) missionaries, (CADR $?MC) cannibals, and the boat to the $?B bank of the river.

```
(THASSERT
  (DEFPROP CROSS
    (THCONSE (MC B DMDC) (MC $?MC $?B)
      (THASSERT (LOOK $?MC $?B))
      (SAFE $?MC)
      (THGOAL (CREW $?DMDC))
      (LE* $?DMDC $?MC)
      (THGOAL (MC $E (MOVE $?MC $?DMDC) $E (OTHER $?B)) (THUSE CROSS))
      (REPORT $?MC $?DMDC $?B)
      (THERASE (LOOK $?MC $?B)))
THEOREM))
```

CROSS carries out the following operations:

1. Assert the state being looked for to prevent an infinite recursive loop.

2. Make sure the state being looked for is safe (no eating).

3. Find an inverse operator (a crew). Remember, each operator is its own inverse.

4. Make sure this inverse operator applies.

5. Find a way to get to the resulting state.

6. Use the automatic popping of the recursive stack to print the solution branch from start state to goal state.

7. Erase what was asserted in step 1, so that no garbage is left over.

(SAFE MC)

MC is a list of the number of missionaries and the number of cannibals on one bank. This function returns NIL if either bank has at least one missionary and more cannibals than missionaries. Otherwise, it returns T.

```
(DEFPROP SAFE
 (LAMBDA (MC)
  (OR (ZEROP (CAR MC)) (EQ (CAR MC) MAX) (EQ (CAR MC) (CADR MC))))
EXPR)
```

(LE* X Y)

X and Y are each lists of two numbers. This function returns T if neither element of X is greater than the respective element of Y.

```
(DEFPROP LE*
 (LAMBDA (X Y)
  (AND (NOT (GREATERP (CAR X) (CAR Y)))
       (NOT (GREATERP (CADR X) (CADR Y)))))
EXPR)
```

(MOVE X DX)

If X is the number of missionaries and cannibals on one bank and DX is the number of missionaries and cannibals that leave that bank, MOVE returns the number of missionaries and cannibals that result on the other bank.

```
(DEFPROP MOVE
 (LAMBDA (X DX)
  (LIST (PLUS MAX (MINUS (CAR X)) (CAR DX))
        (PLUS MAX (MINUS (CADR X)) (CADR DX))))
EXPR)
```

(OTHER SIDE)

If SIDE is the name of one bank, OTHER returns the name of the other bank.

```
(DEFPROP OTHER
 (LAMBDA (SIDE)
  (COND ((EQ SIDE 'LEFT) 'RIGHT) (T 'LEFT)))
EXPR)
```

(REPORT MC DMDC B)

Prints a report of a state and the operator that is applied to that state.

```
(DEFPROP REPORT
  (LAMBDA (MC DMDC B)
    (PRIN3 HAVE *(CAR (MOVE MC DMDC )) MISSIONARIES/,
              *(CADR (MOVE MC DMDC)) CANNIBALS AND
              BOAT ON *(OTHER B) BANK) <>
              *(CAR DMDC) MISSIONARIES AND
              *(CADR DMDC) CANNIBALS CROSS <>))
EXPR)
```

In the LISP we are using, "/" is the escape character that causes the following character to be included in the print name of an atom.

To execute the program, we first assert the operators.

```
(THASSERT (CREW (0 1)))
(THASSERT (CREW (0 2)))
(THASSERT (CREW (1 0)))
(THASSERT (CREW (2 0)))
(THASSERT (CREW (1 1)))
```

Next, we assert the start state.

```
(THASSERT (MC (3 3) LEFT))
```

Finally, we ask if a way can be found to get three missionaries and three cannibals and the boat over to the right bank.

```
(THGOAL (MC (3 3) RIGHT) (THUSE CROSS))
```

The output is as follows:

```
HAVE 3 MISSIONARIES, 3 CANNIBALS AND BOAT ON LEFT BANK
1 MISSIONARIES AND 1 CANNIBALS CROSS
HAVE 1 MISSIONARIES, 1 CANNIBALS AND BOAT ON RIGHT BANK
1 MISSIONARIES AND 0 CANNIBALS CROSS
HAVE 3 MISSIONARIES, 2 CANNIBALS AND BOAT ON LEFT BANK
0 MISSIONARIES AND 2 CANNIBALS CROSS
```

```
HAVE 0 MISSIONARIES, 3 CANNIBALS AND BOAT ON RIGHT BANK
0 MISSIONARIES AND 1 CANNIBALS CROSS
HAVE 3 MISSIONARIES, 1 CANNIBALS AND BOAT ON LEFT BANK
2 MISSIONARIES AND 0 CANNIBALS CROSS
HAVE 2 MISSIONARIES, 2 CANNIBALS AND BOAT ON RIGHT BANK
1 MISSIONARIES AND 1 CANNIBALS CROSS
HAVE 2 MISSIONARIES, 2 CANNIBALS AND BOAT ON LEFT BANK
2 MISSIONARIES AND 0 CANNIBALS CROSS
HAVE 3 MISSIONARIES, 1 CANNIBALS AND BOAT ON RIGHT BANK
0 MISSIONARIES AND 1 CANNIBALS CROSS
HAVE 0 MISSIONARIES, 3 CANNIBALS AND BOAT ON LEFT BANK
0 MISSIONARIES AND 2 CANNIBALS CROSS
HAVE 3 MISSIONARIES, 2 CANNIBALS AND BOAT ON RIGHT BANK
1 MISSIONARIES AND 0 CANNIBALS CROSS
HAVE 1 MISSIONARIES, 1 CANNIBALS AND BOAT ON LEFT BANK
1 MISSIONARIES AND 1 CANNIBALS CROSS

(MC (3 3) RIGHT)
```

Projects

2.1   Change the eight queens program so that it finds all solutions.

2.2   Generalize the missionary and cannibal program so that it will solve the problem with nm missionaries, nc cannibals, and a boat that requires ncn rowers and holds no more than ncm people.

2.3   Write a MICROPLANNER state space program to solve any of the water jug problems of project 1.1.4. Note that these operators are not uniquely reversible. Try representing each operator as a separate consequent theorem.

2.4   Write a MICROPLANNER state space program to solve the Tower of Hanoi problem stated in project 1.1.5.

2.5   Write a state space program using the techniques of Chapter 1.1 to solve the eight queens problem.

2.6   Write a state space program using the techniques of Chapter 1.1 to solve the missionary-cannibal problem.

Chapter 3

Game Playing

3.1 Alpha-Beta Game Tree Searching

Readings: Nilsson, 1971–pp. 137-150
Jackson, 1974–pp. 117-138
Hunt, 1975–pp. 243-252
Raphael, 1976–pp. 86-95
Winston, 1977–Chapter 4

The basic minimax algorithm for evaluating a node of a game tree is as follows:

1. If the node represents a terminal state of the game or is past the depth limit, give the node a number indicating how valuable it is for us (the good guys).

2. Otherwise, if the node represents a state with us to move (a maximizing node), evaluate all its successor nodes and assign this node the maximum of those values.

3. Otherwise, the node represents a state with them to move (a minimizing node). Evaluate all the successor nodes and assign this node the minimum of those values.

The alpha-beta procedure is a more efficient version of the above algorithm based on the following ideas. As the successors of a maximizing (minimizing) node are evaluated, set the PBV (provisional backed-up value) of the node to the maximum (minimum) value found so far. Note that the PBV of a maximizing (minimizing) node never decreases (increases). Let the alpha value of a node be the maximum PBV of its maximizing ancestors, and let the beta value be the minimum PBV of its minimizing ancestors. As soon as the PBV of a maximizing (minimizing) node is greater (less) than or equal to its beta (alpha) value, it is obvious (prove it!) that this node will not be included in the chosen continuation of some ancestor node. We can then stop evaluating its successor nodes and return its current PBV as its final value. This is known as performing a beta (alpha) cutoff.

The following are the core functions for searching a game tree with the alpha-beta algorithm. We will assume the existence of some data structure called a NODE, which will contain information about a state of the game space. Since the depth limit of the search might be changed in various runs of a game-playing program, we assume the level of the root of the tree will be the current depth bound and each node will have a level equal to 1 less than that of its parent.

After presenting the core functions, we will list the functions that need to be defined to play a specific game.

(SEARCH NODE LEVEL ALPHA BETA)

Searches the node NODE that is at level LEVEL and has alpha value ALPHA and beta value BETA. Returns the value of NODE as determined by the search.

```
(DEFPROP SEARCH
  (LAMBDA  (NODE LEVEL ALPHA BETA)
   (PROG2  (SETQ NODE (START NODE))
           (COND ((DEAD NODE LEVEL) (STATIC NODE))
                 (T (SEARCH1 (MAXER NODE)
                             (SUB1 LEVEL)
                             ALPHA
                             BETA
                             (EXPAND NODE))))
           (END NODE)))
 EXPR)
```

The purpose of (SETQ NODE (START NODE)) is that sometimes the state is not stored in a node when it is created, but only the move. The state is then initialized when we start searching the node. Any clean-up that needs to be done when finished with the node is done by (END NODE). SEARCH returns the value calculated in the COND.

The first COND pair determines if we have reached a terminal node. Otherwise, we use SEARCH1 to search down the list of successors. If it is desirable to order the successors, change (EXPAND NODE) to (ORDER (EXPAND NODE)). For forward pruning, make it (PRUNE (ORDER (EXPAND NODE)) LEVEL). Include LEVEL as an argument to PRUNE to allow tapered forward pruning.

(SEARCH1 MAXR LVL ALPHA BETA NL)

Initializes the search of the successors of some node. MAXR is T or NIL depending on whether the parent node is a maximizer or a minimizer. ALPHA and BETA are the alpha and beta values of the parent node. NL is a list of the successor nodes, and LVL is their level.

```
(DEFPROP SEARCH1
 (LAMBDA (MAXR LVL ALPHA BETA NL)
  (SEARCH2 MAXR
           LVL
           ALPHA
           BETA
           (CDR NL)
           (SEARCH (CAR NL) LVL ALPHA BETA)))
EXPR)
```

The last argument of SEARCH2 is a recursive call to SEARCH with the first successor node so that a provisional backed up value is established. Note that the first successor of a node is always searched.

(SEARCH2 MAXR LVL ALPHA BETA NL PBV)

Searches the successors of some node, returning its final backed up value. MAXR, LVL, ALPHA, and BETA are as in SEARCH1. PBV is the provisional backed-up value of the parent node. NL is a list of the still to be searched successor nodes.

```
(DEFPROP SEARCH2
 (LAMBDA (MAXR LVL ALPHA BETA NL PBV)
  (COND ((NULL NL) PBV)
        ((CUTOFF MAXR PBV ALPHA BETA) PBV)
        (T (SEARCH2 MAXR
                    LVL
                    ALPHA
                    BETA
                    (CDR NL)
                    (COND (MAXR
                           (MAX PBV
                                (SEARCH (CAR NL)
                                        LVL
                                        (MAX ALPHA PBV)
                                        BETA)))
                          (T (MIN PBV
                                  (SEARCH (CAR NL)
                                          LVL
                                          ALPHA
                                          (MIN BETA PBV)))))))))
EXPR)
```

Note the order of the first two COND pairs. If all successors have been searched, we do not consider a cutoff to have taken place even if the PBV is appropriate for a cutoff. The main work of SEARCH2 is done in a double recursion. A recursive call to SEARCH to search the next successor and a recursive call to SEARCH2 to search the rest of the successors. PBV is adjusted appropriately in the last argument of SEARCH2, as is alpha or beta for descendants of the next successor. Note that alpha and beta for the node being searched is not changed.

```
(CUTOFF MAXR PBV ALPHA BETA)
```

PBV, ALPHA, and BETA are, respectively, the provisional backed up value, alpha value, and beta value of some node. MAXR is T or NIL depending on whether the node is a maximizing or minimizing node. CUTOFF returns T if searching below the node should be terminated and PBV returned as the final backed up value, and returns NIL otherwise.

```
(DEFPROP CUTOFF
 (LAMBDA (MAXR PBV ALPHA BETA)
  (COND   (MAXR (GE PBV BETA)) (T  (LE PBV ALPHA)))))
EXPR)
```

BETA in the original call to SEARCH should be some large integer, INFINITY. ALPHA should be -INFINITY. If the value of a winning position is also INFINITY, CUTOFF will cause searching below a node to be terminated once a winning move is discovered under the philosophy that one win is as good as another. This is not always true! In the 1971 Computer Chess Tournament, COKO III chose the first move of a mate in two over a mate in one for eight consecutive moves and finally lost the game (see Newborn, 1975, pp. 84-86).

Game Specific Functions To Be Added

```
(START NODE)
```

Does whatever is necessary to prepare for searching the node NODE. NODE is returned, altered if necessary.

```
(END NODE)
```

Does whatever clean-up is necessary after node NODE has been searched.

```
(MAXER NODE)
```

Returns T if NODE is a maximizing node, NIL otherwise. It depends on the representation chosen for NODES.

(DEAD NODE LEVEL)

Returns T if NODE is to be a terminal node of the search tree. Can make use of level information, e.g., (ZEROP LEVEL), as well as information on the state of the game.

(STATIC NODE)

Returns the static value of NODE.

(EXPAND NODE)

Returns a list of the successor nodes of NODE.

3.2 A Program for a Specific Game: Kalah

Kalah is an African game played on a board with twelve "pots" and two "kalahs," half of which belong to the player (us) and half to the opponent (them). When the game begins, each pot contains N "stones" (usually $N = 6$, but it can be any positive integer). The initial board is shown in the figure from the point of view of the opponent since we (represented by the program) will want to be nice when showing the board to the human opponent. Our pots are labeled P1–P6 and the opponent's O1–O6. Our kalah is Pkalah and theirs is Okalah.

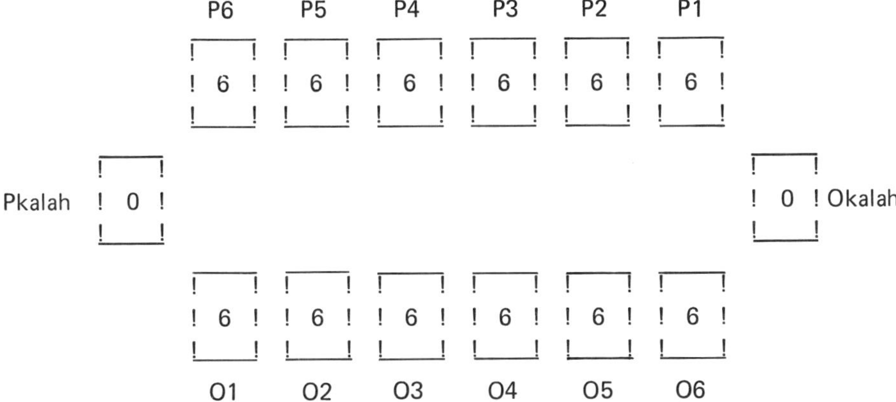

Either side may go first. On their move, a side picks up all the stones in any of their nonempty pots and beginning with the next (counterclockwise) pot or kalah, drops one stone in each of their pots, in their kalah, and in their opponent's pots (but not in the opponent's kalah) until all the stones are distributed.

There are three possible endings to a move:

1. If the last stone is dropped into the moving side's kalah, they go again.
2. If the last stone is dropped into an empty pot owned by the moving side and if the opponent's pot directly across from it is not empty, all the stones from

these two pots are "captured" and placed in the moving side's kalah. The opponent goes next.

3. In all other cases nothing special happens and the opponent goes next.

As soon as one side gets more than half the stones ($6N+1$) in their kalah, the game is over and they win. If it ever happens that all the pots on one side are empty (after either side's move), all the stones in the other side's pots go into that side's kalah, the game is over, and the one with the most stones wins.

Functions Defining the Representation of the Board

We will use one global data structure to represent the board. Each pot and kalah will be represented by an atom. Using the property lists of the atoms, we will make a circular list for each player to use to drop stones, and each pot will have a link to its opposite pot. Since the board will be global, we will use stacks for the number of stones in each pot and kalah for the recursive tree search.

(OTHER PL)

Assuming that PL represents one player, OTHER returns the atom representing the other player.

```
(DEFPROP OTHER
 (LAMBDA (PL) (COND ((EQ PL 'P) 'O) (T 'P)))
EXPR)
```

We use P to represent the program and O to represent the opponent.

(POTR PL N)

Returns the atom representing player PL's Nth pot.

```
(DEFPROP POTR
 (LAMBDA (PL N) (READLIST (LIST PL N)))
EXPR)
```

The program's pots are P1, P2, P3, P4, P5, and P6. The opponent's pots are O1, O2, O3, O4, O5, and O6.

(OWNER POT)

Returns the atom representing the owner of pot POT.

```
(DEFPROP OWNER
 (LABMDA (POT) (CAR (EXPLODE POT)))
EXPR)
```

```
(NUM POT)
```

Returns the number of the pot POT.

```
(DEFPROP NUM
 (LAMBDA (POT) (CADR (EXPLODE POT)))
EXPR)
```

Note that (POTR (OWNER POT) (NUM POT)) = POT.

```
(KALAHR PL)
```

Returns the atom representing player PL's kalah.

```
(DEFPROP KALAHR
 (LAMBDA (PL)
  (COND ((EQ PL 'P) 'PKALAH) (T 'OKALAH)))
EXPR)
```

The program's kalah is represented by PKALAH, the opponent's by OKALAH.

```
(VALUE POT)
```

Returns the number of stones in the pot POT.

```
(DEFPROP VALUE
 (LAMBDA (POT) (CAR (GET POT 'KVALUE)))
EXPR)
```

The number of stones in a pot is stored on the property list of the atom representing the pot as CAR of the list, which is the value of the property KVALUE. This list is used as a stack.

```
(PUSHVAL POT VAL)
```

Stacks VAL as the current number of stones in the pot POT. Previous values are maintained further down in the stack.

```
(DEFPROP PUSHVAL
 (LAMBDA (POT VAL)
  (PUT POT 'KVALUE (CONS VAL (GET POT 'KVALUE))))
EXPR)
```

```
(POPVAL POT)
```

Pops the stack used to maintain the value of pot POT, restoring the previous value.

```
(DEFPROP POPVAL
 (LAMBDA (POT)
  (PUT POT 'KVALUE (CDR (GET POT 'KVALUE))))
EXPR)
```

```
(CHANGEVAL POT VAL)
```

Changes the current value of pot POT to VAL, destroying the previous current value.

```
(DEFPROP CHANGEVAL
 (LAMBDA (POT VAL)
  (PUT POT 'KVALUE (CONS VAL (CDR (GET POT 'KVALUE)))))
EXPR)
```

```
(EMPTY POT)
```

Returns T if there are no stones in pot POT, NIL otherwise.

```
(DEFPROP EMPTY
 (LAMBDA (POT) (ZEROP (VALUE POT)))
EXPR)
```

```
(PATHR POT)
```

Returns the name of one of the two circular paths connecting the pots and kalahs:

PPATH   The path the program uses to drop its stones.
OPATH   The path the opponent uses to drop his stones.

```
(DEFPROP PATHR
 (LAMBDA (PL)
```

```
    (COND ((EQ PL 'P) 'PPATH) (T 'OPATH)))
EXPR)
```

(SIDER PL)

Returns a list of all the pots on player PL's side of the board.

```
(DEFPROP SIDER
 (LAMBDA (PL)
  (COND    ((EQ PL 'P)'(P1 P2 P3 P4 P5 P6))
          (T '(O1 O2 O3 O4 O5 O6)))))
EXPR)
```

(SETPATH P LAT)

Joins each atom in the list LAT to the next one via the path P.

```
(DEFPROP SETPATH
 (LAMBDA (P LAT)
  (COND    ((NULL (CDR LAT)) NIL)
          ((PUT (CAR LAT) P (CADR LAT)) (SETPATH P (CDR LAT)))))
EXPR)
```

To initialize the paths for the kalah board, do the following:

(SETPATH 'PPATH '(P1 P2 P3 P4 P5 P6 PKALAH O1 O2 O3 O4 O5 O6 P1))

and

(SETPATH 'OPATH '(O1 O2 O3 O4 O5 O6 OKALAH P1 P2 P3 P4 P5 P6 O1))

(OPP POT)

Returns the pot opposite POT on the board.

```
(DEFPROP OPP
 (LAMBDA (POT) (GET POT 'OPP))
EXPR)
```

(SETSYM P LAT LAT2)

Joins corresponding atoms of the two lists, LAT and LAT2 to each other symmetrically via the path P.

```
(DEFPROP SETSYM
 (LAMBDA (P LAT LAT2)
   (COND   ((NULL LAT) NIL)
           ((NULL LAT2) NIL)
           ((PUT (CAR LAT) P (CAR LAT2))
            (PUT (CAR LAT2) P (CAR LAT))
            (SETSYM P (CDR LAT) (CDR LAT2)))))
EXPR)
```

To initialize the OPP relations, do the following:

```
(SETSYM 'OPP '(P1 P2 P3 P4 P5 P6) '(O6 O5 O4 O3 O2 O1))
```

Functions to Define the Legal Moves

(MOVE PL POT)

Makes the move, representing player PL moving the stones in pot POT, and changes the global board representation accordingly. It returns T if player PL gets to go again, NIL otherwise.

```
(DEFPROP MOVE
 (LAMBDA (PL POT) (MOVE1 PL POT (TAKE POT) (PATHR PL) (KALAHR PL)))
EXPR)
```

(MOVE1 PL POT STONES PATH KALAH)

Player PL moves STONES number of stones taken from pot POT along the path PATH. KALAH is PL's kalah. It returns T if PL gets to go again, NIL otherwise.

```
(DEFPROP MOVE1
 (LAMBDA (PL POT STONES PATH KALAH)
  (PROG NIL
        (REPEAT UNTIL (ZEROP STONES)
                (SETQ POT (GET POT PATH))
                (DROP 1 POT)
                (SETQ STONES (SUB1 STONES)))
        (CHECKCAP POT PL KALAH (OPP POT))
        (CHECKMT)
        (RETURN (EQ POT KALAH))))
EXPR)
```

A move consists of the following:

    1. Dropping the stones one at a time in each pot along the proper path.

2. Making a capture, if appropriate.

3. Emptying all the pots on one side into that side's kalah, if the other side has become empty.

The same player gets to go again if and only if his last stone landed in his kalah.

(CHECKCAP POT PL KALAH OPPOT)

Player PL, whose kalah is KALAH, has just moved, the last stone landing in pot POT. OPPOT is the pot opposite POT. CHECKCAP checks to see if this move was a capture move, and, if so, makes the capture.

```
(DEFPROP CHECKCAP
 (LAMBDA (POT PL KALAH OPPOT)
  (COND
   ((AND   (EQ (VALUE POT) 1)
           (EQ (OWNER POT) PL)
           (NOT (EQ POT KALAH))
           (NOT (EMPTY OPPOT)))
    (DROP (TAKE POT) KALAH)
    (DROP (TAKE OPPOT) KALAH))))
EXPR)
```

(CHECKMT)

If all the pots on either side are empty, all the pots on the other side are emptied into that side's kalah.

```
(DEFPROP CHECKMT
 (LAMBDA NIL
  (COND ((MTSIDEP (SIDER 'P)) (MTSIDE (SIDER 'O) 'OKALAH))
        ((MTSIDEP (SIDER 'O)) (MTSIDE (SIDER 'P) 'PKALAH))))
EXPR)
```

(MTSIDEP SIDE)

Returns T if all pots in the list SIDE are empty, NIL otherwise.

```
(DEFPROP MTSIDEP
 (LAMBDA (SIDE)
  (REPEAT UNTIL (NULL SIDE)
```

```
                WHILE (EMPTY (CAR SIDE))
                      (SETQ SIDE (CDR SIDE)))))
EXPR)
```

(MTSIDE SIDE KALAH)

Removes the stones from all pots in the list SIDE and puts them in KALAH.

```
(DEFPROP MTSIDE
 (LAMBDA (SIDE KALAH)
  (MAPC (FUNCTION (LAMBDA (P) (DROP (TAKE P) KALAH)))
        SIDE))
EXPR)
```

(TAKE POT)

Removes all the stones from pot POT and returns the number of stones removed.

```
(DEFPROP TAKE
 (LAMBDA (POT) (PROG2 NIL (VALUE POT) (CHANGEVAL POT 0))))
EXPR)
```

(DROP N POT)

Adds N stones to pot POT.

```
(DEFPROP DROP
 (LAMBDA (N POT) (CHANGEVAL POT (PLUS N (VALUE POT)))))
EXPR)
```

Functions to Define the Nodes of the Game Tree

A node will be represented by a list of three elements. When a node is first generated, the first element will be the player who is to move, the second element will be the pot whose stones are to be taken, and the third element will be the player who will move next. After the move is made by the function START, the node will be reversed, so that the first element will be the player to move next and the third element will be the player who made the last move. A node represents a multiple move if the first and third elements are equal.

```
(DEFPROP PLAYER
 (LAMBDA (NODE) (CAR NODE))
EXPR)

(DEFPROP MOVEOF
 (LAMBDA (NODE) (CADR NODE))
EXPR)

(DEFPROP MULT
 (LAMBDA (NODE) (EQ (CAR NODE) (CADDR NODE)))
EXPR)
```

Functions Required for Searching the Game Tree

These are the game specific functions listed at the end of Sec. 3.1.

```
(START NODE)
```

When we start to search the node NODE, we must stack the current contents of the board, make the move represented by NODE, and return the reverse of NODE as mentioned above.

```
(DEFPROP START
 (LAMBDA (NODE)
  (PROG NIL
   (MAPC  (FUNCTION (LAMBDA (P) (PUSHVAL P (VALUE P))))
          '(P1 P2 P3 P4 P5 P6 PKALAH O1 O2 O3 O4 O5 O6 OKALAH))
   (MOVE (PLAYER NODE) (MOVEOF NODE))
   (RETURN (REVERSE NODE)))))
EXPR)
```

```
(END NODE)
```

The only thing that need be done when we have finished evaluating a node is to restore the board to its previous condition by popping the values of the pots and kalahs.

```
(DEFPROP END
 (LAMBDA (NODE)
  (MAPC (FUNCTION POPVAL)
        (P1 P2 P3 P4 P5 P6 PKALAH O1 O2 O3 O4 O5 O6 OKALAH)))
EXPR)
```

(DEAD NODE LEVEL)

Returns T if NODE is to be a terminal node of the search tree. LEVEL will be greater than 0 if the depth bound has not yet been reached.

```
(DEFPROP DEAD
 (LAMBDA (NODE LEVEL)
  (OR (AND (LE LEVEL 0) (NOT (MULT NODE)))
      (GREATERP (VALUE 'PKALAH) HALFSTONES)
      (GREATERP (VALUE 'OKALAH) HALFSTONES)
      (AND (EQ (VALUE 'PKALAH) HALFSTONES)
           (EQ (VALUE 'OKALAH) HALFSTONES))))
EXPR)
```

This will be a terminal node if we have reached the level bound and we are not in the midst of a multiple move, or if the game is over.

(STATIC NODE)

Returns the static value of NODE.

```
(DEFPROP STATIC
 (LAMBDA (NODE)
  (PROG2 (SETQ TNODES (ADD1 TNODES))
         (COND
          ((GREATERP (VALUE 'PKALAH) HALFSTONES) INFINITY)
          ((GREATERP (VALUE 'OKALAH) HALFSTONES) (MINUS INFINITY))
          (T (DIFFERENCE (VALUE 'PKALAH) (VALUE 'OKALAH))))))
EXPR)
```

The static value will just be the difference in kalahs, unless the game is won or lost. TNODES is used to keep count of the number of terminal nodes evaluated, so that statistics can be printed.

(MAXER NODE)

Returns T if the node is a maximizing node, NIL otherwise.

```
(DEFPROP MAXER
 (LAMBDA (NODE) (EQ (PLAYER NODE) 'P))
EXPR)
```

(EXPAND NODE)

Returns a list of the successor nodes of NODE.

```
(DEFPROP EXPAND
 (LAMBDA (NODE)
  (PROG2 (SETQ BNODES (ADD1 BNODES))
         (EXPAND1 (PLAYER NODE) (SIDER (PLAYER NODE)))))
EXPR)
```

BNODES is used to keep count of the number of nodes expanded.

(EXPAND1 PL SIDE)

Returns a list of nodes representing the moves player PL can make from the current state of the board. SIDE is a list of PL's pots.

```
(DEFPROP EXPAND1
 (LAMBDA (PL SIDE)
  (PROG (LMULT LCAP LREG)
        (MAPC (FUNCTION
               (LAMBDA (POT)
                 (COND ((EMPTY POT) NIL)
                       ((MULTMOVE POT)
                        (SETQ LMULT (CONS (LIST PL POT PL) LMULT)))
                       ((CAPMOVE POT)
                        (SETQ LCAP
                              (CONS (LIST PL POT (OTHER PL)) LCAP)))
                       (T (SETQ LREG
                                (CONS (LIST PL POT (OTHER PL))
                                      LREG))))))
              SIDE)
        (RETURN (APPEND LMULT LCAP LREG)))))
EXPR)
```

Moves can only be made from nonempty pots. The list of possible moves is ordered: multiple moves, capture moves, others. This is done to try to play a strong game and to try to maximize cutoffs.

(MULTMOVE POT)

Returns T if a move from pot POT will result in the player making the move getting another turn, NIL otherwise.

```
(DEFPROP MULTMOVE
 (LAMBDA (POT)
  (EQ (REMAINDER (VALUE POT) 13) (DIFFERENCE 7 (NUM POT)))))
EXPR)
```

If s is the number of stones in the player's nth pot, the last stone will land in the player's kalah if and only if

$$s \bmod 13 = 7 - n.$$

(CAPMOVE PL POT)

Returns T if player PL's move from pot POT will result in a capture of some stones.

```
(DEFPROP CAPMOVE
 (LAMBDA (PL POT) (CAPMOVE 1 PL POT (VALUE POT) (NUM POT)))
EXPR)
```

(CAPMOVE1 PL POT V N)

Returns T if PL's move from POT will result in a capture, NIL otherwise. POT is PL's Nth pot and it has V stones in it.

```
(DEFPROP CAPMOVE1
 (LAMBDA (PL POT V N)
  (OR (EQ V 13)
      (AND (LESSP V (DIFFERENCE 7 N))
           (ZEROP (VALUE (POTR PL (PLUS N V))))
           (NOT (EMPTY (OPP (POTR PL (PLUS N V))))))
      (AND (GREATERP V (DIFFERENCE 13 N))
           (LESSP V 13)
           (EMPTY (POTR PL (PLUS N-13 V))))))
EXPR)
```

If V = 13, the last stone will land in POT, and the opposite pot must have at least one stone in it, since one will be dropped into it on this move. If $V < (7 - N)$, the last stone will land in PL's pot number N+V. We must check that it is empty and that the pot opposite it is not. If $(13 - N) < V < 13$, the last stone will land in PL's pot number N + V - 13, and we must check that it is now empty, but PL will drop a stone into all the opponent's pots, so none of them will be empty. In all other cases, a capture will not occur.

Functions for Controlling an Interactive Game

(KALAH N DEPTH)

This function is used to begin a game with the program. N is the number of stones in each pot at the beginning of the game. DEPTH is the depth bound on the search.

```
(DEFPROP KALAH
 (LAMBDA (N DEPTH)
  (PROG NIL
        (INITBRD N)
        (PRINTBRD)
        (ALTMOVE (MEFIRST?))
        (RETURN 'THANKS)))
EXPR)
```

(INITBRD VAL)

Initializes the board by putting VAL stones in each pot and emptying the two kalahs. Also, it initializes the global variable HALFSTONES.

```
(DEFPROP INITBRD
 (LAMBDA (VAL)
  (PROG NIL
        (SETQ HALFSTONES (TIMES VAL 6))
        (MAPC (FUNCTION
                (LAMBDA (POT) (PUT POT 'KVALUE (LIST VAL))))
              '(P1 P2 P3 P4 P5 P6 O1 O2 O3 O4 O5 O6))
        (DEFPROP PKALAH (0) KVALUE)
        (DEFPROP OKALAH (0) KVALUE)))
EXPR)
```

(PRINTBRD)

Does a formatted print of the current state of the board.

```
(DEFPROP PRINTBRD
 (LAMBDA NIL
  (PRIN3 < > %7
        ! 7 C ! *(VALUE 'P6)  ! ! 7 C ! *(VALUE 'P5)  !
        ! 7 C ! *(VALUE 'P4)  ! ! 7 C ! *(VALUE 'P3)  !
        ! 7 C ! *(VALUE 'P2)  ! ! 7 C ! *(VALUE 'P1)  !
        < >
```

```
      ! 7 C !   *(VALUE 'PKALAH)  !   %42
      ! 7 C !   *(VALUE 'OKALAH)  !
      <> %7
      ! 7 C !   *(VALUE 'O1)  ! ! 7 C !  *(VALUE 'O2)  !
      ! 7 C !   *(VALUE 'O3)  ! ! 7 C !  *(VALUE 'O4)  !
      ! 7 C !   *(VALUE 'O5)  ! ! 7 C !  *(VALUE 'O6)  !
      <> ))
EXPR)
```

(MEFIRST?)

Asks if the opponent wants to go first. Returns T if the program should go first, NIL otherwise.

```
(DEFPROP MEFIRST?
 (LAMBDA NIL
  (PROG (ANS)
       (RETURN
         (REPEAT (PRIN3 DO YOU WANT TO GO FIRST?)
                 (SETQ ANS (READ))
           WHILE  (NOT (EQ ANS 'YES))
           UNTIL  (EQ ANS 'NO)
                 (PRIN3 PLEASE ANSWER YES OR NO <>)))))
EXPR)
```

(ALTMOVE P?)

Alternates moves between the program and the opponent until the game is over. P? is T if the program should go first, NIL otherwise.

```
(DEFPROP ALTMOVE
 (LAMBDA (P?)
  (COND (P? (REPEAT UNTIL (PMOVE)
                   UNTIL (ENDGAME)
                   UNTIL (OMOVE)
                   UNTIL (ENDGAME)))
        (T (REPEAT UNTIL (OMOVE)
                   UNTIL (ENDGAME)
                   UNTIL (PMOVE)
                   UNTIL (ENDGAME)))))
EXPR)
```

(OMOVE)

Gets the opponent's move, makes it, and prints the resulting board until either it is no longer the opponent's move or the game is over. It returns T if the game is over, NIL if it is now the program's move. In the latter case, the game might or might not be over.

```
(DEFPROP OMOVE
  (LAMBDA NIL
    (REPEAT WHILE (PROG2 NIL (MOVE 'O (GETMOVE)) (PRINTBRD))
          UNTIL (ENDGAME)
                (PRIN3 YOU GO AGAIN <>)))
EXPR)
```

(GETMOVE)

Interacts with the opponent, returning the pot the opponent chooses to move, making sure it is a legal move.

```
(DEFPROP GETMOVE
  (LAMBDA NIL
    (PROG (N)
        (REPEAT (PRIN3 WHAT'S YOUR MOVE?)
                (SETQ N (READ))
          UNTIL  (AND (NUMBERP N)
                      (GREATERP N 0)
                      (LESSP N 7)
                      (NOT (EMPTY (POTR 'O N))))
                (PRIN3 <> THAT'S ILLEGAL <>))
        (RETURN (POTR 'O N))))
EXPR)
```

(ENDGAME)

If the game is over, this function prints an appropriate message and returns T; otherwise it returns NIL.

```
(DEFPROP ENDGAME
  (LAMBDA NIL
    (COND
    ((GREATERP (VALUE 'PKALAH) HALFSTONES) (PRIN3 I WIN <>))
    ((GREATERP (VALUE 'OKALAH) HALFSTONES) (PRIN3 YOU WIN <>))
    ((AND (EQ (VALUE 'PKALAH) HALFSTONES)
          (EQ (VALUE 'OKALAH) HALFSTONES))
```

```
    (PRIN3    IT'S A TIE <>))
   (T NIL)))
EXPR)
```

===

```
(PMOVE)
```

Causes the program to make moves until either it is the opponent's turn or the game ends. It returns T if the game is over, NIL if it is now the opponent's move. In the latter case, the game might or might not be over.

```
(DEFPROP PMOVE
 (LAMBDA NIL
  (PROG2 (PRIN3 I GO <>)
         (REPEAT (PRIN3 HMMM/././.)
                 WHILE (PLAY 0 0 (TIME))
                 UNTIL (ENDGAME)
                 (PRIN3 I GO AGAIN <>)))))
EXPR)
```

===

```
(PLAY BNODES TNODES SECS)
```

Makes a move for the program. BNODES is the number of nodes expanded so far. TNODES is the number of terminal nodes evaluated. SECS is the number of CPU milliseconds used so far by the program. This function returns T if the program gets another move.

```
(DEFPROP PLAY
 (LAMBDA (BNODES TNODES SECS) (PLAY1 (EXPAND '(P NIL NIL))))
EXPR)
```

===

```
(PLAY1 LNODES)
```

LNODES is a list of possible moves. PLAY1 chooses one of them and makes it, returning T if the program gets another move.

```
(DEFPROP PLAY1
 (LAMBDA (LNODES)
  (CHOOSE (CDR LNODES)
          (CAR LNODES)
          (COND ((CDR LNODES)
                 (SEARCH (CAR LNODES) DEPTH ALPHA BETA))
                (T 'NOT/ CALCULATED))))
EXPR)
```

If there is only one possible move, no search is done.

(CHOOSE LNODES BEST V)

Chooses and makes the best possible move. BEST is the best move found so far, V is its value, LNODES is a list of alternative moves. It returns T if the program gets another move.

```
(DEFPROP CHOOSE
 (LAMBDA (LNODES BEST V)
  (PROG (NV)
       (REPEAT WHILE LNODES
               UNTIL (EQ V INFINITY)
               (SETQ NV (SEARCH (CAR LNODES) DEPTH V BETA))
               (COND
                ((GREATERP NV V) (SETQ V NV)
                                 (SETQ BEST (CAR LNODES)))))
               (SETQ LNODES (CDR LNODES)))
       (RETURN (MAKE BEST V))))
EXPR)
```

(MAKE CHOSEN VAL)

Makes the move, CHOSEN, whose value is VAL, reports to the opponent and prints the board. It returns T if the program gets another move.

```
(DEFPROP MAKE
 (LAMBDA (CHOSEN VAL)
  (PROG2 (REPORT (NUM (MOVEOF CHOSEN))
                VAL
                BNODES
                TNODES
                (DIFFERENCE (TIME) SECS))
        (MOVE (PLAYER CHOSEN) (MOVEOF CHOSEN))
        (PRINTBRD)))
EXPR)
```

(REPORT M V B T S)

Reports to the opponent that move M was chosen, it had a calculated value of V, B nodes were expanded, T terminal nodes were evaluated, and S CPU msec were used to make the decision.

```
(DEFPROP REPORT
 (LAMBDA (M V B T S)
  (PRIN3 <>I MOVE *M VALUE *V <>
       *B EXPANDED *T EVALUATED *S MILLISECS <>))
 EXPR)
```

Example

Let's play a quick game starting with three stones per pot.

```
*(KALAH 3 3)
        3        3        3        3        3        3
0                                                               0
        3        3        3        3        3        3
DO YOU WANT TO GO FIRST?  NO
I GO
HMMM . . .
I MOVE 6 VALUE 6
80 EXPANDED 105 EVALUATED 10838 MILLISECS
        0        3        3        3        3        3
1                                                               0
        4        4        3        3        3        3
WHAT'S YOUR MOVE?  4
        0        3        3        3        3        3
1                                                               1
        4        4        3        0        4        4
YOU GO AGAIN
WHAT'S YOUR MOVE?  1
        0        3        3        3        3        3
1                                                               1
        0        5        4        1        5        4
I GO
HMMM . . .
I MOVE 4 VALUE 5
43 EXPANDED 18 EVALUATED 4284 MILLISECS
        1        4        0        3        3        3
2                                                               1
        0        5        4        1        5        4
I GO AGAIN
HMMM . . .
I MOVE 1 VALUE 8
67 EXPANDED 68 EVALUATED 8253 MILLISECS
        1        4        0        4        4        0
7                                                               1
        0        5        0        1        5        4
```

WHAT'S YOUR MOVE? 2

	1	4	0	4	4	0
7						
	0	0	1	2	6	5

(right: 2)

YOU GO AGAIN
WHAT'S YOUR MOVE? 6

	1	4	1	5	5	1
7						
	0	0	1	2	6	0

(right: 3)

I GO
HMMM . . .
I MOVE 6 VALUE 14
76 EXPANDED 113 EVALUATED 11082 MILLISECS

	0	4	1	5	5	1
8						
	0	0	1	2	6	0

(right: 3)

I GO AGAIN
HMMM . . .
I MOVE 2 VALUE 15
57 EXPANDED 70 EVALUATED 7740 MILLISECS

	1	5	2	6	0	1
9						
	0	0	1	2	6	0

(right: 3)

I GO AGAIN
HMMM . . .
I MOVE 6 VALUE 15
41 EXPANDED 34 EVALUATED 4929 MILLISECS

	0	5	2	6	0	1
10						
	0	0	1	2	6	0

(right: 3)

I GO AGAIN
HMMM . . .
I MOVE 1 VALUE 12
36 EXPANDED 38 EVALUATED 4477 MILLISECS

	0	5	2	6	0	0
17						
	0	0	1	2	0	0

(right: 3)

WHAT'S YOUR MOVE? 3

	0	5	2	6	0	0
17						
	0	0	0	3	0	0

(right: 3)

I GO
HMMM . . .
I MOVE 4 VALUE 12
19 EXPANDED 14 EVALUATED 2030 MILLISECS

```
          1          6          0          6          0          0
17                                                                        3
          0          0          0          3          0          0
WHAT'S YOUR MOVE?  4
          1          6          0          6          0          0
17                                                                        4
          0          0          0          0          1          1
YOU GO AGAIN
WHAT'S YOUR MOVE?  6
          1          6          0          6          0          0
17                                                                        5
          0          0          0          0          1          0
YOU GO AGAIN
WHAT'S YOUR MOVE?  5
          1          6          0          6          0          0
17                                                                        5
          0          0          0          0          0          1
I GO
HMMM . . .
I MOVE 6 VALUE 1000
2 EXPANDED 1 EVALUATED 147 MILLISECS
          0          6          0          6          0          0
18                                                                        5
          0          0          0          0          0          1
I GO AGAIN
HMMM . . .
I MOVE 5 VALUE 1000
1 EXPANDED 1 EVALUATED 71 MILLISECS
          1          0          0          6          0          0
19                                                                        5
          1          1          1          1          0          1
I WIN
THANKS
```

Projects

3.1   As now written, the Kalah program searches the game tree before each move of a
multiple move. Is this necessary? If it is, demonstrate that. If it is not necessary,
prove it and modify the program so that it no longer does it.

3.2   Modify the Kalah program to use some pruning heuristics, thereby allowing it to
search deeper in the tree. Also explore different orderings in EXPAND2.

3.3   Write a program to play Konane (Hawaiian checkers). This is played on an 8 x 8
board of dark and light pieces as shown (using X for dark and O for light).

```
        1 2 3 4 5 6 7 8

    8   X O X O X O X O
    7   O X O X O X O X
    6   X O X O X O X O
    5   O X O X O X O X
    4   X O X O X O X O
    3   O X O X O X O X
    2   X O X O X O X O
    1   O X O X O X O X
```

First, the dark player removes a dark piece either at position 18, 81, 45, or 54. Next the light player removes a light piece adjacent to the space created by the first move. Then the players alternate moves, each jumping one of his/her own pieces over one horizontally or vertically adjacent opponent piece, landing in a space on the other side, and removing the jumped piece. If desired, this may be continued in a multiple move, as long as the same piece is moved in a straight line.

For example, after the following moves:

dark	light
removes 54	removes 55
(34 54)	(57 55)
(32 34)	(52 32)
(76 56)	(64 66)
(78 76)	(24 44 64)

the board looks like

```
        1 2 3 4 5 6 7 8

    8   X O X O X O X O
    7   O X O X O X . .
    6   X O X O X O X O
    5   O . O . O X . X
    4   X . X . X O X O
    3   O X . . O X O X
    2   X O X . X O X O
    1   O X O X O X O X
```

The first player who cannot make a legal move loses.

For further discussion of this game, see Gyllenskog (1976).

Chapter 4

Theorem Proving

4.1 Wang's Algorithm

Readings: Raphael, 1976–pp. 111-119
Wang, 1960

Wang's algorithm for proving theorems of propositional calculus is essentially the falsification method. It uses two lists of formulas, LL and LR, which we write as LL ==> LR. The formulas in LL have the truth value TRUE. Those in LR have the truth value FALSE. The basic operation is to assign subformulas to LL or LR as required by the truth value of the formula of which they are a part. In some cases a "straight line" reduction can be carried out. For example if (P & Q) is in LL, both P and Q must be in LL. In other cases a "splitting" reduction is required. If (P & Q) is in LR, we must investigate both P being in LR and Q being in LR.

To determine if a formula is a theorem, place it in LR and carry out the above operation until either all atomic formulas have been assigned a unique truth value or there is no way to carry out the operation without assigning both truth values to the formula. In the former case, the formula was not a theorem. In the latter case it was.

We will represent formulas in infix notation using

$$\begin{array}{ll}
\neg & \text{for negation} \\
\& & \text{for conjunction} \\
! & \text{for disjunction} \\
=> & \text{for conditional} \\
<=> & \text{for biconditional}
\end{array}$$

and we will fully parenthesize the formulas.

We will represent each line of the proof by a datatype called LINE with fields LVL, LA, LF, RA, and RF.

```
(DATA LINE (LVL LA LF RA RF))
```

The fields are used as follows:

LVL	An integer that increases by 1 for each "splitting."
LA	The atomic formulas in LL.
LF	The nonatomic formulas in LL.
RA	The atomic formulas in LR.
RF	The nonatomic formulas in LR.

```
(PROVE "WFF")
```

Prints a proof or falsification of the formula WFF. It returns T if WFF is a theorem, NIL if not.

```
(DEFPROP PROVE
 (LAMBDA (WFF) (WANG (ADDR (CAR WFF) (LINE 0 NIL NIL NIL NIL))))
FEXPR)
```

```
(WANG L)
```

Prints the line L and a proof or falsification of L. Returns T if L cannot be falsified, NIL if it can.

```
(DEFPROP WANG
 (LAMBDA (L)
  (PROG2 (PRINLINE L)
        (COND  ((PRIM-NO L) NIL)
               ((PRIM-YES L) T)
               ((NULL (LF L))
                (REDR (CAR (RF L)) (RF L (CDR (RF L)))))
               (T (REDL (CAR (LF L)) (LF L (CDR (LF L)))))))))
EXPR)
```

```
(PRIM-NO L)
```

If the line L consists of only atomic formulas and none of them are in both LA and RA, this function prints "NOT VALID" and returns T. Otherwise, it returns NIL.

```
(DEFPROP PRIM-NO
 (LAMBDA (L)
  (COND
   ((AND (NULL (LF L)) (NULL (RF L)) (DISJOINT (LA L) (RA L)))
```

```
    (PRIN3 % (LVL L) NOT VALID <>))
    (T NIL)))
EXPR)
```

```
(PRIM-YES L)
```

If the line L has some formula on both the right and left sides, this function prints "IS VALID" and returns T. Otherwise, it returns NIL.

```
(DEFPROP PRIM-YES
 (LAMBDA (L)
  (COND
   ((NOT (AND (DISJOINT (LA L) (RA L)) (DISJOINT (LF L) (RF L))))
    (PRIN3 % (LVL L) IS VALID <>))
   (T NIL)))
EXPR)
```

```
(DISJOINT LA LB)
```

If the lists LA and LB have no top level elements in common, this function returns T. Otherwise, it returns NIL.

```
(DEFPROP DISJOINT
 (LAMBDA (LA LB)
  (COND   ((NULL LA) T)
          ((MEMBER (CAR LA) LB) NIL)
          (T (DISJOINT (CDR LA) LB))))
EXPR)
```

```
(REDL WFF L)
```

Reduces the line (LF L (CONS WFF (LF L))) according to the main propositional connective in the formula WFF. It returns T if that line is valid, NIL if it is falsifiable.

```
(DEFPROP REDL
 (LAMBDA (WFF L)
  (COND
   ((EQ (CAR WFF) '¬) (WANG (ADDR (CADR WFF) L)))
   ((EQ (CADR WFF) '&)
    (WANG (ADDL (CAR WFF) (ADDL (CADDR WFF) L))))
   ((EQ CADR WFF) '!)
    (AND (WANG (ADDL (CAR WFF) (BUMP L)))
```

```
                (WANG (ADDL (CADDR WFF) (BUMP L)))))
      ((EQ (CADR WFF) '=>)
       (AND (WANG (ADDL (CADDR WFF) (BUMP L)))
                (WANG (ADDR (CAR WFF) (BUMP L)))))
      ((EQ (CADR WFF) '<=>)
       (AND (WANG (ADDL (CAR WFF) (ADDL (CADDR WFF) (BUMP L))))
                (WANG (ADDR (CAR WFF) (ADDR (CADDR WFF) (BUMP L)))))))))
EXPR)
```

(REDR WFF L)

Reduces the line (RF L (CONS WFF (RF L))) according to the main propositional
connective in the formula WFF. It returns T if that line is valid, NIL if it is falsifiable.

```
(DEFPROP REDR
 (LAMBDA (WFF L)
  (COND
   ((EQ (CAR WFF) '¬) (WANG (ADDL (CADR WFF) L)))
   ((EQ (CADR WFF) '=>)
    (WANG (ADDL (CAR WFF) (ADDR (CADDR WFF) L))))
   ((EQ (CADR WFF) '!)
    (WANG (ADDR (CAR WFF) (ADDR (CADDR WFF) L))))
   ((EQ (CADR WFF) '&)
    (AND (WANG (ADDR (CAR WFF) (BUMP L)))
            (WANG (ADDR (CADDR WFF) (BUMP L)))))
   ((EQ (CADR WFF) '<=>)
    (AND (WANG (ADDL (CAR WFF) (ADDR (CADDR WFF) (BUMP L))))
            (WANG (ADDL (CADDR WFF) (ADDR (CAR WFF) (BUMP L)))))))))
EXPR)
```

(ADDL WFF L)

Adds the formula WFF to the left side of the line L.

```
(DEFPROP ADDL
 (LAMBDA (WFF L)
  (COND ((ATOM WFF) (LA L (INSERT WFF (LA L))))
        (T (LF L (INSERT WFF (LF L))))))
EXPR)
```

WFF is not added if it already occurs on the left side of L. It is added to LA if it is an
atomic formula, to LF if it is nonatomic.

(ADDR WFF L)

Adds the formula WFF to the right side of the line L.

```
(DEFPROP ADDR
 (LAMBDA (WFF L)
  (COND ((ATOM WFF) (RA L (INSERT WFF (RA L))))
        (T (RF L (INSERT WFF (RF L))))))
EXPR)
```

WFF is not added if it already occurs on the right side of L. It is added to RA if it is an atomic formula, to RF if it is nonatomic.

===

(BUMP L)

Increments the level of the line L.

```
(DEFPROP BUMP
 (LAMBDA (L) (LVL L (PLUS 2 (LVL L))))
EXPR)
```

===

(PRINLINE L)

Prints the line L in a nice format.

```
(DEFPROP PRINLINE
 (LAMBDA (L)
  (PROG NIL
          (PRIN3 % (LVL L))
          (PRLST (LA L))
          (PRLST (LF L))
          (PRIN3 ===>)
          (PRLST (RA L))
          (PRLST (RF L))
          (PRIN3 <>)))
EXPR)
```

===

(PRLST L)

Prints the list L without the outer parentheses.

```
(DEFPROP PRLST
 (LAMBDA (L) (EVALQUOTE (FUNCTION PRIN3) L))
EXPR)
```

Example

As an example, we show the proof of one of deMorgan's Laws:
(PROVE ((¬ (P & Q)) < = >((¬P) ! (¬Q))))

```
===> (( ¬ (P & Q)) <=>(( ¬ P) ! ( ¬ Q)))
   ( ¬ (P & Q))===> (( ¬ P) ! ( ¬ Q))
   ===> (P & Q) (( ¬ P) ! ( ¬ Q))
      ===> P (( ¬P) ! ( ¬ Q))
      ===>P ( ¬ P) ( ¬ Q)
      P ===>P ( ¬ Q)
      IS VALID
      ===>Q (( ¬P) ! ( ¬ Q))
      ===>Q ( ¬P) ( ¬Q)
      P ===>Q ( ¬Q)
      Q P ===>Q
      IS VALID
   (( ¬ P) ! ( ¬ Q)) ===> ( ¬ (P & Q))
      ( ¬P)===> ( ¬ (P & Q))
      ===> P ( ¬ (P & Q))
      (P & Q)===> P
      P Q ===> P
      IS VALID
      ( ¬Q)===> ( ¬ (P & Q))
      ===> Q ( ¬ (P & Q))
      (P & Q)===>Q
      P Q ===> Q
      IS VALID
T
```

Projects

4.1.1 Change the Wang Algorithm program so that "straight line" reductions are done before "splitting" reductions.

  (*Hint:* Add two more fields to LINE.)

4.2 The Resolution Method

Readings: Chang and Lee, 1973—pp. 70-97
          Hunt, 1975—pp. 287-343
          Jackson, 1974—Chapter 6
          Raphael, 1976—pp. 120-134

The resolution method is a mechanical theorem-proving technique that operates on a set of "clauses," each of which is a set of "literals." A literal is an atomic proposition or the negation of an atomic proposition. A clause represents the disjunction of its literals with all variables universally quantified.

The basic resolution operation is the "clash" of two clauses, producing another clause, which is then added to the set of clauses. If one clause contains a literal that is the negation of a literal in another clause, they may be clashed producing a clause containing the union of the two clauses with the literal and its negation deleted. For example, ((F X) (¬ (G Y (F Y))) clashes with ((¬ (F X)) (H Z)) to produce ((¬ (G Y (F Y))) (H Z)). This can be seen to be equivalent to the deduction of ((G Y (F Y)) = >(H Z)) from ((G Y (F Y)) = > (F X)) and ((F X) = >(H Z)). Similarly, the clash of two clauses, one of which contains only one literal, is equivalent to Modus Ponens. It is, of course, permissible to transform a clause by renaming its variables to get it into clashable form. The unification algorithm of Robinson (1965) prepares two clauses for clashing in the "most general" way.

To prove that a conclusion formula is deducible from a set of assumption formulas by resolution, one does a type of proof by contradiction. Take the assumptions and the negation of the conclusion, transform them into clauses, and clash away. If this is done in an organized fashion and the conclusion does in fact follow from the assumptions, the empty clause will eventually be produced. Much research has gone into finding ways of making this search for the null clause more efficient.

We present here a program that can be given a list of premises and a conclusion and will print a proof that the conclusion follows from the premises using the resolution method. The proof will be a numbered list of clauses, showing how each clause was derived. If the conclusion did follow from the premises, the last clause printed will be NIL. If the conclusion did not follow from the premises, the program may discover this or may run forever.

Input to the program will be as fully parenthesized formulas using infix notation, as in Sec. 4.1. Quantified formulas will look like:

((A X) (P X))   for universal quantification
((E X) (P X))   for existential quantification

So that we can identify clauses by line number, we will use a data type, LCLAUSE, consisting of a LINE number and a CLAUSE.

(DATA LCLAUSE (LINE CLAUSE))

(PROVE PREMISES CONCLUSION)

Takes a list of PREMISES and a CONCLUSION and prints a numbered list of clauses a) derived from the premises, b) derived from the negation of the conclusion, c) derived from previous clauses by resolution. If PROVE terminates, it will return T if the conclusion followed from the premises or NIL if it did not. If CONCLUSION is NIL, step (b) will be left out, and PROVE will test if the premises are contradictory.

```
(DEFPROP PROVE
  (LAMBDA (PREMISES CONCLUSION)
   (PROG (NCL CLS)
         (SETQ NCL 0)
         (REPEAT
           WHILE PREMISES
                 (SETQ CLS
                       (APPEND (LIST-CLS (CLAUSEFORM (CAR PREMISES)))
                                       'PREMISE)
                               CLS))
                 (SETQ PREMISES (CDR PREMISES)))
         (COND (CONCLUSION
                (SETQ CLS
                      (APPEND
                       (LIST-CLS (CLAUSEFORM (LIST ' ¬ CONCLUSION))
                                'CONCLUSION)
                       CLS))))
         (RETURN (RESOLVE CLS)))))
EXPR)
```

(LIST-CLS CLS TYPE)

CLS is a list of clauses derived according to the reason, TYPE. LIST-CLS returns a list of LCLAUSEs formed from these clauses and prints these LCLAUSEs in numerical order.

```
(DEFPROP LIST-CLS
  (LAMBDA (CLS TYPE)
   (PROG    (LCLS)
            (REPEAT
              WHILE CLS
                    (SETQ NCL (ADD1 NCL))
                    (SETQ LCLS (CONS (LCLAUSE NCL (CAR CLS)) LCLS))
                    (PRIN3 *NCL * (CAR CLS) *TYPE <>)
                    (SETQ CLS (CDR CLS)))
            (RETURN LCLS)))
EXPR)
```

Functions Defining the Structure and Coding of Formulas

(OP WFF)

Returns the main propositional connective or quantifier clause of the formula, WFF, if it has one. Otherwise, it returns NIL.

```
(DEFPROP OP
 (LAMBDA (WFF)
  (COND ((ATOM WFF) NIL)
        ((NULL (CDR WFF)) NIL)
        ((NULL (CDDR WFF))
         (COND
          ((OR (NEG? (CAR WFF)) (QUANTIFIER? (CAR WFF))) (CAR WFF))
          (T NIL)))
        ((MEMBER (CADR WFF) '(! & => <=>)) (CADR WFF))
        (T NIL)))
EXPR)
```

(OR? OP)

Returns T if OP is the symbol used for disjunction; NIL otherwise.

```
(DEFPROP OR?
 (LAMBDA (OP) (EQ OP '!))
EXPR)
```

(AND? OP)

Returns T if OP is the symbol used for conjunction, NIL otherwise.

```
(DEFPROP AND?
 (LAMBDA (OP) (EQ OP '&))
EXPR)
```

(NEG? OP)

Returns T if OP is the symbol used for negation, NIL otherwise.

```
(DEFPROP NEG?
 (LAMBDA (OP) (EQ OP '¬))
EXPR)
```

(COND? OP)

Returns T if OP is the symbol used for conditional, NIL otherwise.

```
(DEFPROP COND?
 (LAMBDA (OP) (EQ OP '=>))
EXPR)
```

(BICOND? OP)

Returns T if OP is the symbol used for biconditional, NIL otherwise.

```
(DEFPROP BICOND?
 (LAMBDA (OP) (EQ OP '<=>))
EXPR)
```

(QUANTIFIER? C)

Returns T if C is a quantifier clause, NIL otherwise.

```
(DEFPROP QUANTIFIER?
 (LAMBDA (C) (AND (NOT (ATOM C)) (MEMBER (CAR C) '(A E))))
EXPR)
```

Functions to Change Formulas into Clauses

(CLAUSEFORM WFF)

Returns a list of the clauses derived from the formula, WFF.

```
(DEFPROP CLAUSEFORM
 (LAMBDA (WFF)
  (CLAUSES
   (CNF (SKOLEMIZE (STANDARDIZE (MINISCOPE (CONDELIM WFF)))))))
EXPR)
```

(CLAUSES WFF)

Returns a list of the clauses derived from the formula, WFF, which is in Skolem-normal and conjunctive-normal form.

```
(DEFPROP CLAUSES
 (LAMBDA (WFF)
  (COND  ((AND? (OP WFF))
          (APPEND (CLAUSES (CAR WFF)) (CLAUSES (CADDR WFF))))
         ((OR? (OP WFF)) (LIST (CLAUSE-IT WFF)))
         (T (LIST (LIST WFF)))))
EXPR)
```

(CLAUSE-IT WFF)

Returns a clause derived from the formula WFF, which is a disjunction of literals.

```
(DEFPROP CLAUSE-IT
 (LAMBDA (WFF)
  (COND   ((OR? (OP WFF))
           (APPEND (CLAUSE-IT (CAR WFF)) (CLAUSE-IT (CADDR WFF))))
          (T (LIST WFF))))
EXPR)
```

(CONDELIM WFF)

Returns the formula WFF with conditionals and biconditionals eliminated, re-placing occurrences of (A => B) by ((¬ A) ! B), and occurrences of (A <=> B) by ((A ! (¬B)) & ((¬ A) ! B)).

```
(DEFPROP CONDELIM
 (LAMBDA (WFF) (CONDELIM1 WFF (OP WFF)))
EXPR)

(DEFPROP CONDELIM1
 (LAMBDA (WFF OP)
  (COND   ((NULL OP) WFF)
          ((OR (QUANTIFIER? OP) (NEG? OP))
           (LIST (CAR WFF) (CONDELIM (CADR WFF))))
          ((COND? OP)
           (LIST (LIST ' ¬ (CONDELIM (CAR WFF)))
                 '!
                 (CONDELIM (CADDR WFF))))
          ((BICOND? OP)
           (LIST (LIST (CONDELIM (CAR WFF))
                       '!
                       (LIST ' ¬ (CONDELIM (CADDR WFF))))
                 '&
                 (LIST (LIST ' ¬ (CONDELIM (CAR WFF)))
                       '!
                       (CONDELIM (CADDR WFF)))))
          (T (LIST (CONDELIM (CAR WFF))
                   (CADR WFF)
                   (CONDELIM (CADDR WFF))))))
EXPR)
```

(MINISCOPE WFF)

Returns the formula WFF, which has no conditionals or biconditionals, with all negations driven in to minimum scope.

```
(DEFPROP MINISCOPE
 (LAMBDA (WFF) (MINISCOPE1 WFF (OP WFF)))
EXPR)

(DEFPROP MINISCOPE1
 (LAMBDA (WFF OP)
  (COND  ((NULL OP) WFF)
         ((QUANTIFIER? OP) (LIST (CAR WFF) (MINISCOPE (CADR WFF))))
         ((NEG? OP) (NEGATE (CADR WFF)))
         (T (LIST (MINISCOPE (CAR WFF))
                  (CADR WFF)
                  (MINISCOPE (CADDR WFF))))))
EXPR)
```

(NEGATE WFF)

Returns the negation of the formula WFF, which has no conditionals or biconditionals.

```
(DEFPROP NEGATE
 (LAMBDA (WFF) (NEGATE1 WFF (OP WFF)))
EXPR)

(DEFPROP NEGATE1
 (LAMBDA (WFF OP)
  (COND  ((AND? WFF) '!)
         ((OR? WFF) '&)
         ((NULL OP) (LIST ' ¬ WFF))
         ((NEG? OP) (MINISCOPE (CADR WFF)))
         ((QUANTIFIER? OP)
          (LIST (CONS (COND ((EQ (CAR OP) 'A) 'E) (T 'A))
                      (CDR OP))
                (NEGATE (CADR WFF))))
         (T (MAPCAR (FUNCTION NEGATE) WFF))))
EXPR)
```

(STANDARDIZE WFF)

Returns the formula WFF with its variables renamed so that no two quantifiers quantify variables with the same print names.

```
(DEFPROP STANDARDIZE
 (LAMBDA (WFF) (STANDARDIZE1 WFF (OP WFF)))
EXPR)

(DEFPROP STANDARDIZE1
 (LAMBDA (WFF OP)
   (COND  ((NULL OP) WFF)
          ((QUANTIFIER? OP)
           (SUBST (NEWVAR)
                  (CADR OP)
                  (LIST OP (STANDARDIZE (CADR WFF)))))
          (T (MAPCAR (FUNCTION STANDARDIZE) WFF))))
EXPR)
```

Initially variables are recognized because they are precisely the things that are bound by quantifiers.

(NEWVAR)

Returns a variable that has never been used before in this run of the program.

```
(DEFPROP NEWVAR
 (LAMBDA NIL
  (PROG (V) (SETQ V (GENSYM)) (PUT V 'VAR T) (RETURN V)))
EXPR)
```

A new variable is marked by putting the pair (VAR T) on its property list for later identification.

(SKOLEMIZE WFF)

Returns the formula WFF in Skolem-normal form. WFF must have no conditionals or biconditionals, must be in miniscope form, and must have its variables standardized.

```
(DEFPROP SKOLEMIZE
 (LAMBDA (WFF) (SKOLEM1 NIL WFF (OP WFF)))
EXPR)
```

(SKOLEM1 VARS WFF OP)

Returns the formula WFF, whose main connective is OP, in Skolem-normal form. WFF must satisfy the conditions given above. Each existentially quantified variable in WFF is a function of all the variables in the list VARS as well as any other universally quantified variables in whose scope it is.

```
(DEFPROP SKOLEM1
 (LAMBDA (VARS WFF OP)
  (COND   ((NULL OP) WFF)
          ((QUANTIFIER? OP)
           (COND ((EQ (CAR OP) 'A)
                   (SKOLEM1 (SNOC VARS (CADR OP))
                            (CADR WFF)
                            (OP (CADR WFF))))
                 (T (SKOLEM1 VARS
                             (SUBST (CONS (GENSYM) VARS)
                                    (CADR OP)
                                    (CADR WFF))
                             (OP (CADR WFF))))))
          (T (MAPCAR (FUNCTION (LAMBDA(X) (SKOLEM1 VARS X (OP X))))
                     WFF))))
EXPR)
```

(CNF WFF)

Returns the formula WFF in conjunctive-normal form. WFF must be in mini-scope form, have no quantifiers, and have only the connectives &, !, and ¬ .

```
(DEFPROP CNF
 (LAMBDA (WFF)
   (COND ((ATOM WFF) WFF) (T (CNF1 (MAPCAR (FUNCTION CNF) WFF)))))
EXPR)
```

(CNF1 WFF)

Returns the formula WFF in conjunctive-normal form. If WFF is not a literal, both operands of its main connective must already be in conjunctive-normal form.

```
(DEFPROP CNF1
 (LAMBDA (WFF)
   (COND ((OR? (OP WFF)) (DISTRIB (CAR WFF) (CADDR WFF)))
         (T WFF)))
EXPR)
```

(DISTRIB F1 F2)

Returns a formula equivalent to (F1 ! F2), but in conjunctive-normal form. Both F1 and F2 must be in conjunctive-normal form.

```
(DEFPROP DISTRIB
 (LAMBDA (F1 F2)
  (COND
   ((AND? (OP F1))
    (LIST (DISTRIB (CAR F1) F2) '& (DISTRIB (CADDR F1) F2)))
   ((AND? (OP F2))
    (LIST (DISTRIB F1 (CAR F2)) '& (DISTRIB F1 (CADDR F2))))
   (T (LIST F1 '! F2))))
EXPR)
```

Functions to Apply Resolution to a List of Clauses

(RESOLVE OPEN)

generates new clauses from OPEN, which is a list of LCLAUSEs. It returns T as soon as the null clause is generated , and returns NIL if no more clauses can be generated and the null clause has not been produced. RESOLVE uses Level-Saturation, a simple breadth-first search through the clauses. Each clause is printed as it is generated.

```
(DEFPROP RESOLVE
 (LAMBDA (OPEN)
  (PROG    (CLOSED NEW)
           (RETURN
             (REPEAT
                WHILE OPEN
                       (SETQ NEW (TRY-CLASHES (RENAME (CAR OPEN))
                       CLOSED))
                UNTIL  (NIL-ON NEW)
                       (SETQ CLOSED (CONS (CAR OPEN) CLOSED))
                       (SETQ OPEN (CDR (APPEND OPEN NEW)))))))))
EXPR)
```

(RENAME LCL)

Changes the CLAUSE field of the LCLAUSE LCL by renaming its variables. Returns the new LCLAUSE.

```
(DEFPROP RENAME
 (LAMBDA (LCL)
  (CLAUSE LCL
          (APPLY-SUBST (MAPCAR (FUNCTION
                                (LAMBDA (X) (CONS X (NEWVAR))))
                               (VBLS (CLAUSE LCL)))
```

```
                                        (CLAUSE LCL))))
EXPR)
```

```
(VBLS CL)
```

Returns a list of the variables in the clause CL.

```
(DEFPROP VBLS
 (LAMBDA (CL)
  (COND   ((NULL CL) NIL)
          ((VARIABLE? (CAR CL)) (INSERT (CAR CL) (VBLS (CDR CL))))
          ((ATOM (CAR CL)) (VBLS (CDR CL)))
          (T (MERGE1 (VBLS (CAR CL)) (VBLS (CDR CL))))))
EXPR)
```

```
(VARIABLE? A)
```

Returns T if the atom A is a variable generated by (NEWVAR). Otherwise, returns NIL.

```
(DEFPROP VARIABLE?
 (LAMBDA (A) (GET A 'VAR))
EXPR)
```

```
(NIL-ON L)
```

Returns T if the first LCLAUSE on L, a list of LCLAUSEs, has the null clause as its CLAUSE. Otherwise, returns NIL.

```
(DEFPROP NIL-ON
 (LAMBDA (L) (COND (L (NULL (CLAUSE (CAR L)))) (T NIL)))
EXPR)
```

```
(TRY-CLASHES CL LCL)
```

Returns a list of all the LCLAUSES produced by clashing the LCLAUSE CL against the LCLAUSEs in the list LCL. If the null clause is generated, TRY-CLASHES returns immediately with the null clause as the first LCLAUSE on the list.

```
(DEFPROP TRY-CLASHES
 (LAMBDA (CL LCL)
  (PROG   (NEWCLS)
```

```
    (REPEAT
        WHILE LCL
                (SETQ NEWCLS
                        (APPEND (TRY-CLASH CL (CAR LCL)) NEWCLS))
        UNTIL (NIL-ON NEWCLS)
                (SETQ LCL (CDR LCL)))
    (RETURN NEWCLS)))
EXPR)
```

(TRY-CLASH CL1 CL2)

Returns a list of LCLAUSEs produced by clashing the LCLAUSE CL1 against the LCLAUSE CL2 and causes these LCLAUSEs to be printed. If the null clause is produced, it will be first on the list returned.

```
(DEFPROP TRY-CLASH
  (LAMBDA (CL1 CL2)
    (LIST-CLS (TRY-CLASH1 (CLAUSE CL1) (CLAUSE CL2))
            (LIST 'R (LINE CL1) (LINE CL2)))))
EXPR)
```

(TRY-CLASH1 CL1 CL2)

Returns a list of all clauses produced by clashing clause CL1 against clause CL2, but returns immediately if the null clause is generated with it as the first clause on the list.

```
(DEFPROP TRY-CLASH1
  (LAMBDA (CL1 CL2)
    (PROG (CCL1 CCL2 F1 F2 S NEWCLS)
            (SETQ CCL1 CL1)
            (REPEAT
            WHILE CCL1
                    (SETQ F1 (CAR CCL1))
                    (SETQ CCL1 (CDR CCL1))
                    (SETQ CCL2 CL2)
            UNTIL  (REPEAT
                        WHILE CCL2
                                (SETQ F2 (CAR CCL2))
                                (SETQ CCL2 (CDR CCL2))
                                (COND
                                ((OR (AND (NEG?  (OP F1))
                                            (NULL  (OP F2))
                                            (SETQ S (UNIFY (CADR F1) F2)))
                                    (AND (NULL (OP F1))
```

```
                                         (NEG? OP F2))
                                         (SETQ S (UNIFY F1 (CADR F2)))))
                         (SETQ NEWCLS
                            (CONS
                             (MERGE
                              (APPLY-SUBST S (REMOVE* F1 CL1))
                              (APPLY-SUBST S (REMOVE* F2 CL2)))
                             NEWCLS))))
                   UNTIL (AND NEWCLS (NULL (CAR NEWCLS)))))
          (RETURN NEWCLS)))
  EXPR)
```

(REMOVE* S L)

Returns the list L with all occurrences of the S-expression S removed.

```
(DEFPROP REMOVE*
 (LAMBDA (S L)
  (COND   ((NULL L) NIL)
          ((EQUAL S (CAR L)) (REMOVE* S (CDR L)))
          (T (CONS (CAR L) (REMOVE* S (CDR L))))))
 EXPR)
```

(MERGE L1 L2)

Returns a list containing all the expressions that occur as top-level members of either the list L1 or the list L2. The returned list contains no element more than once, although L1 or L2 might.

```
(DEFPROP MERGE
 (LAMBDA (L1 L2) (MERGE1 L1 (MERGE1 L2 NIL)))
 EXPR)
(DEFPROP MERGE1
 (LAMBDA (L1 L2)
  (COND   ((NULL L1) L2) (T (INSERT (CAR L1) (MERGE1 (CDR L1) L2)))))
 EXPR)
```

Functions for the Unification Algorithm

(UNIFY F1 F2)

Returns the most general unifier of the positive literals F1 and F2, or NIL if they are not unifiable. The most general unifier is a substitution, which is represented by a list of dotted pairs:

                (. . . (variable · term) . . .).

```
(DEFPROP UNIFY
 (LAMBDA (F1 F2)
  (PROG    (SUBS SPAIR)
           (SETQ SUBS '((T . T)))
           (COND
             ((REPEAT
                UNTIL  (EQUAL F1 F2)
                       (SETQ SPAIR (LIST (UNIFY1 F1 F2)))
                WHILE  (CAR SPAIR)
                       (SETQ F1  (APPLY-SUBST SPAIR F1))
                       (SETQ F2  (APPLY-SUBST SPAIR F2))
                       (SETQ SUBS (COMPOSE-SUBST SUBS SPAIR)))
              (RETURN SUBS))
             (T (RETURN NIL)))))
 EXPR)
```

(UNIFY1 F1 F2)

Returns a dotted pair (variable . term), such that the variable does not occur in the term and the variable and term occur in corresponding positions in the two positive literals, F1 and F2. Returns NIL if no such pair can be found.

```
(DEFPROP UNIFY1
 (LAMBDA (F1 F2)
  (COND   ((VARIABLE? F1)
             (COND ((OCCUR-IN F1 F2) NIL) (T (CONS F1 F2))))
          ((VARIABLE? F2)
             (COND ((OCCUR-IN F2 F1) NIL) (T (CONS F2 F1))))
          ((ATOM F1) NIL)
          ((ATOM F2) NIL)
          ((EQ (CAR F1) (CAR F2)) (UNIFY2 (CDR F1) (CDR F2)))
          (T NIL)))
 EXPR)
```

(UNIFY2 A1 A2)

Does the same as UNIFY1, except that A1 and A2 are positive literals with the function names deleted, i. e., they are lists of terms.

```
(DEFPROP UNIFY2
 (LAMBDA (A1 A2)
  (PROG2 (REPEAT
```

```
        WHILE (EQUAL (CAR A1) (CAR A2))
              (SETQ A1  (CDR A1))
              (SETQ A2  (CDR A2)))
     (UNIFY1  (CAR A1)  (CAR A2))))
EXPR)
```

(OCCUR-IN S1 S2)

Returns T if the expression S1 occurs in the expression S2 at any level.

```
(DEFPROP OCCUR-IN
 (LAMBDA (S1 S2)
  (COND  ((EQUAL S1 S2 ) T)
         ((ATOM S2) NIL)
         ((OCCUR-IN S1 (CAR S2)) T)
         (T (OCCUR-IN S1 (CDR S2)))))
EXPR)
```

(APPLY-SUBST SUBST CLAUSE)

Applies the substitution SUBST to the formula CLAUSE, returning the modified formula.

```
(DEFPROP APPLY-SUBST
 (LAMBDA (SUBST CLAUSE)
  (COND ((ATOM CLAUSE)
         (CDR
          (SASSOC CLAUSE
                  SUBST
                  (FUNCTION (LAMBDA NIL (CONS NIL CLAUSE))))))
        (T (CONS (APPLY-SUBST SUBST (CAR CLAUSE))
                 (APPLY-SUBST SUBST (CDR CLAUSE))))))
EXPR)
```

(COMPOSE-SUBST S1 S2)

Returns a substitution that has the same effect as applying first the substitution S1 and then the substitution S2.

```
(DEFPROP COMPOSE-SUBST
 (LAMBDA (S1 S2) (ADDNEW S2 (COMPOSE1 S1 S2)))
EXPR)
```

(COMPOSE1 S1 S2)

Applies the substitution S2 to the terms of the substitution S1, returning the modified S1.

```
(DEFPROP COMPOSE1
 (LAMBDA (S1 S2)
  (COND   ((NULL S1) NIL)
          (T (CONS (CONS (CAAR S1) (APPLY-SUBST S2 (CDAR S1)))
                   (COMPOSE1 (CDR S1) S2)))))
EXPR)
```

(ADDNEW S2 NEWS1)

Adds to the substitution NEWS1 those dotted pairs of the substitution S2 whose variables are not already variables of NEWS1, returning the modified NEWS1.

```
(DEFPROP ADDNEW
 (LAMBDA (S2 NEWS1)
   (COND ((NULL S2) NEWS1)
         ((ASSOC (CAAR S2) NEWS1) (ADDNEW (CDR S2) NEWS1))
         (T (CONS (CAR S2) (ADDNEW (CDR S2) NEWS1)))))
EXPR)
```

Example

As an example, we will prove that Socrates is mortal.

```
*(PROVE '(((A X) ((HUMAN X) = > (MORTAL X))) (HUMAN SOCRATES))
         '(MORTAL SOCRATES))

1  (( ¬ (HUMAN G0006)) (MORTAL G0006)) PREMISE
2  ((HUMAN SOCRATES)) PREMISE
3  (( ¬ (MORTAL SOCRATES))) CONCLUSION
4  ((MORTAL SOCRATES)) (R 1 2)
5  (( ¬ (HUMAN SOCRATES))) (R 1 3)
6  NIL (R 5 2)
T
```

Projects

4.2.1 Add factoring to the program of this section. In this process, literals within a clause are unified and resulting duplicate literals are deleted. For example, the clause ((P X Y) (P Z C) (P W D)) may be factored into ((P V C) (P W D)), where X, Y, Z, W, V are variables. Without factoring, resolution is not complete (curiously, because of renaming). For example, try to derive the null clause with renaming, but without factoring from ((P X) (P Y)) and (($\neg$ (P X)) ($\neg$ (P Y))).

4.2.2   Add to the program of this section the deletion strategy in which tautologies and subsumed clauses are deleted as soon as they are generated. A tautology is a clause containing both a literal and its own negation. A clause D is subsumed by another clause C, if there is a substitution S, such that all the literals of (APPLY-SUBST S C) are in D.

4.2.3   Add some ordering strategies to the program of this section, such as unit preference and set of support.

Chapter 5

Pattern Recognition and Vision

5.1 Pattern Recognition

Readings: Hunt, 1975—Chapters 4, 5, 8
              Uhr, 1973—Chapters 2-5

SNOBOL4 References: Gimpel, 1976
                        Griswold, 1972
                        Griswold, 1975
                        Griswold and Griswold, 1973
                        Griswold et al., 1971
                        Maurer, 1976

The pattern recognition techniques of whole template, partial template, n-tuples, meaningful features, etc. may be seen as the same program that applies a series of "characterizers" or "feature detectors" to the input and makes a decision based on which ones were found. We may write this as a SNOBOL4 program, taking advantage of the SNOBOL4 backtracking pattern-match algorithm.

The functions in this section are presented as they would be prepared for a SNOBOL4 run: an asterisk in column 1 indicating a comment.

*   We will use a set of feature detectors Di, each of which has a pattern Pi, a
* weight Wi, and a list of implications. Each implication consists of a class name Cj and a
* weight Wij. If Pi is in the input, the program will add $Wi * Wij$ to a tally for each Cj.

*   We may use a programmer-defined data type for the feature detectors:

```
DATA('DETECTOR (PATTERN, WEIGHT, IMPLIED, NEXT) ')
```

* where the fields are:

*   PATTERN   The feature that is to be matched to the input. The program
*   will do the different styles of character recognition mentioned
*   above depending on the kind of pattern placed in this field.

```
*       WEIGHT         A weighting factor for this characterizer.
*       IMPLIED        A list of classes and weights implied by this feature's being
*                      recognized in the input.
*       NEXT           The next detector in a list of detectors.
```

```
****************************************************************************
```

```
*       The implied list is made up of nodes of another data type:
```

DATA('IMPLICATION (CLASS, WEIGHT, IMPLIED) ')

```
*  These fields are:
```

```
*       CLASS          The implied class.
*       WEIGHT         A weighting factor for the implication.
*       IMPLIED        The next node in the implied list.
```

```
****************************************************************************
```

```
*       We can now define the core recognition functions.
```

DEFINE('RECOGNIZE (INSTANCE, DETECTORS) VOTES')

```
*       INSTANCE is a SNOBOL4 string representing an input to be classified.
*  DETECTORS is a list of DETECTOR types to be used.  VOTES will be a TABLE
*  for tallying the votes for the possible classes.  RECOGNIZE will return the name of
*  the class chosen.
```

```
                                                    : (RECOGNIZE_END)
RECOGNIZE           VOTES = TABLE( )
RECOGNIZE.1         RECOGNIZE = IDENT(DETECTORS)
+                          WINNER (CONVERT(VOTES, 'ARRAY'))
                                                    : S (RETURN)
+                  INSTANCE PATTERN(DETECTORS)
+                   = ADD. VOTES (IMPLIED(DETECTORS),
+                   WEIGHT (DETECTORS), VOTES)
                   DETECTORS = NEXT(DETECTORS)   : (RECOGNIZE.1)
RECOGNIZE_END
```

```
*  Note that the INSTANCE is never changed since ADD.VOTES (which is only called
*  if the pattern match succeeds) always fails.
```

```
****************************************************************************
```

DEFINE('ADD.VOTES (IMP, WT, VOTES)')

```
*       IMP is the implied list of a detector whose weight is WT.  VOTES is a table
*  for tallying the votes.  ADD.VOTES updates the entries in VOTES according to
*  IMP and WT, and does a failure return.
```

```
                                                      : (ADD.VOTES_END)
ADD.VOTES           IDENT(IMP)                         : S (FRETURN)
                    VOTES <CLASS (IMP) >= VOTES <CLASS (IMP) >
+                   + WEIGHT(IMP) * WT
                    IMP = IMPLIED(IMP)                 : (ADD.VOTES)
ADD.VOTES_END
*
```

****

DEFINE ('WINNER(BALLOT) SIZE, I, MAX')

*   BALLOT is an array containing the final votes in the following form:
* BALLOT$<I, 1>$ is the name of the Ith class and BALLOT $<I, 2>$ is the number
* of votes received. WINNER returns the name of the first class with the maximum
* number of votes.

ARRAY.SIZE.PAT = BREAK(',') . SIZE

*   ARRAY.SIZE.PAT is a pattern to extract the number of rows from the pro-
* totype of an array and assign it to SIZE.

```
                                                      : (WINNER_END)
WINNER              PROTOTYPE(BALLOT) ARRAY.SIZE.PAT
WINNER.1            I = LT(I, SIZE) I + 1              : F (WINNER.2)
                    MAX = GT(BALLOT <1, 2>,
+                   BALLOT <MAX, 2> ) I                : (WINNER.1)
WINNER.2            WINNER = BALLOT <MAX, 1 >          : (RETURN)
WINNER_END
```

****

Kinds of Patterns

In designing patterns for the detectors, the following pattern valued function is
very useful:

DEFINE ('PATNO(PAT, MIN, MAX)CPAT, I')

*   This function returns a pattern that matches at least MIN and at most MAX
* occurrences of the pattern PAT ($0 \leq$ MIN $\leq$ MAX). The local CPAT will be the
* concatenation of I occurrences of PAT.

```
                                                      : (PATNO_END)
PATNO               I = LT (I, MIN) I + 1              : F (PATNO. 1)
                    CPAT = CPAT PAT                    : (PATNO)
PATNO.1             PATNO = CPAT
```

```
PATNO.2              I = LT(I, MAX) 1 + 1              : F(RETURN)
                     CPAT = CPAT PAT
                     PATNO = PATNO 1 CPAT             : (PATNO.2)
PATNO_END
```

****

In what follows, we will assume that the unknowns to be recognized are represented by a string which has been extracted in row major order from an array with R rows and C columns. For simplification, we will also assume a line drawing with 'X' representing the presence of a line and ' ' representing the absence of a line. For example, the string ' X   XXX X X XXXXXX   X' would represent the 5 by 5 input:

```
* * * * * *
*   X     *
*  XXX    *
*  X X    *
* XXXXX   *
* X     X *
* * * * * *
```

Template recognition involves merely using strings of length R*C as the patterns. Each implication list would then have only one element. A whole template can also be considered to be an R*C-tuple. Smaller tuples are also easy to design. For example a 2-tuple that looks at positions $N+1$ and $M+1$ ($N < M$) in the string involves four detectors with the following patterns:

```
TAB (N) ' ' TAB (M) ' '
TAB (N) ' ' TAB (M) 'X'
TAB (N) 'X' TAB (M) ' '
TAB (N) 'X' TAB (M) 'X'
```

As the positions being looked at become less dependent on absolute position in the string and more dependent on positions relative to each other, we pass into the technique of "features," or even "meaningful features." For example, the pattern

```
MASK1 = ' ' LEN(1) 'X' LEN(C - 2) 'X' LEN(C - 2) 'X' LEN(1) ' '
```

is equivalent to the following "diagonal line feature":

```
-?X
?X?
X?-
```

where '-' must match a ' ', 'X' must match a 'X', and '?' can match either. A pattern that allows this feature to match anywhere in the input is:

```
PATNO(LEN(C), 0, R - 3) PATNO(LEN(1), 0, C - 3) MASK1
```

A pattern that matches this feature anywhere in the lower-left-hand quarter of the input is:

```
PATNO(LEN(C), R  / 2, R  -  3)  PATNO(LEN(1), 0, C  / 2  -  3)  MASK1
```

Note that since we are controlling where MASK1 can match, we should do the pattern matching in anchored mode.

Learning the Weights

The weights, Wi and Wij, may be derived by a training procedure during which the program "looks at" several examples of each class, being "told" the class of each input. How should the weights be calculated?

Assume the program inputs N examples, Nc of which are examples of the class C. Also assume that the feature F is recognized in Nf of the examples, including Nfc examples of C, and $Nf - Nfc$ examples of other classes. If we assume that future examples will have the same statistical distribution as the "learning set," we have the following probabilities. The *a priori* probability of an example's being a C is Nc/N. The *a priori* probability of F matching an example is Nf/N. The probability of F matching given that an example is a C is Nfc/Nc. The probability of an example's being a C given that F matches is Nfc/Nf. It is this last probability that we are interested in using during the "test" or "production" phase of the program. If Wi is $1/Ni$ and Wij is Nij, then this is the quantity that will be calculated in ADD.VOTES.

Functions for Learning the Weights

```
        DEFINE('LEARN (EX, CL, LEARN) FEAT')
```

```
*
        LEARN is a list of detectors whose weights are updated appropriately for the
*
  example EX of class CL.
*

                                             : (LEARN_END)
LEARN            FEAT = DIFFER(LEARN) LEARN   : F (RETURN)
LEARN.1          EX PATTERN(FEAT) = UPDATE(FEAT, CL)
                 FEAT = DIFFER(NEXT(FEAT))
                 NEXT(FEAT)                   : S (LEARN.1)
+                                             F (RETURN)

LEARN_END

*
        Note that EX is never changed because UPDATE always fails.
*
```

```
********************************************************************************
```

```
                          DEFINE('UPDATE(FEAT, CL) ')
*
*        Updates the weights for the feature FEAT and for its implication of the class
*  CL.  UPDATE always returns failure.
*

                                                              : (UPDATE_END)
UPDATE          WEIGHT(FEAT) = IDENT (WEIGHT(FEAT)) 1.
+                                                             : S (UPDATE. 1)
                WEIGHT(FEAT) = 1.  /  (1.  /  WEIGHT(FEAT)  +  1.)
UPDATE. 1       IMPLIED(FEAT) = IDENT(IMPLIED(FEAT))
+                                   IMPLICATION(CL, 1.) : S (FRETURN)


                FEAT = IMPLIED(FEAT)
                WEIGHT(FEAT) = IDENT(CLASS(FEAT), CL)
+                                   WEIGHT(FEAT)+  1.  : S (FRETURN)
                                                          F (UPDATE.1)
+
UPDATE_END
```

<hr>

Projects

5.1.1   Collect a data set of characters by asking a friend to print one character in
each of a set of squares you have drawn on a piece of paper. Draw a grid (say,
20 x 20) over each square and prepare a binary array representing each character. Prepare a data file containing a number of such data sets for use in the
projects below. For each example, the file should contain a representation of
the array and the class name. Use as characters the first one, two, three or
four of the following groups:

    1.   the letters A B D H I O R T
    2.   the letters C E F G J L P Q
    3.   the letters K M N S U V W X Y Z
    4.   the digits 0 1 2 3 4 5 6 7 8 9

5.1.2   Write and try out a complete pattern recognition program on the data collected
for project 5.1.1 with a set of detectors you design. Design the detectors
appropriate to the character classes in your data set, but without considering
the idiosyncrasies of the particular examples in the data file. Try this without
the learning section by programming your own implication lists and setting all
weights to 1. Have your program print a confusion matrix in which it shows
the number of times letters of class C_i were identified as of class C_j, for all
i, j. Also have your program print the percent of examples it identified cor-
rectly. Discuss the reasons for any mistakes your program made.

5.1.3   Do project 5.1.2 including learning the weights. Start with a list of detectors with empty implication lists. Divide the data file into a learning set and a test set. Learn the weights using only the learning set. Then test your program on both the learning set and the test set, printing separate statistics and confusion matrices for each set. Again, discuss the results, including why the program got 100% of the learning set correct—or why it didn't.

5.1.4   This same program can simulate a trainable organism. Consider the classes to be behaviors in the repertoire of the organism, and pattern instances to be stimuli. Input a stimulus to the program and it will output a behavior response. Then input a reward or punishment. A reward should increase the weight of the implied behavior on all detectors that matched. Punishment should decrease these weights. Implement this idea and experiment with it.

5.1.5   Extend the program from project 5.1.4 by providing it with a memory of its own previous N actions (for some N). Include this memory with the next stimulus. Use operant conditioning to train your program to perform some behavior sequences.

5.2 Edge and Vertex Finding

Readings: Jackson, 1975—Chapter 5
Winston, 1975a—Chapters 2, 3
Winston, 1977—Chapters 3, 8

In this section, we go through the first few steps in identifying edges, vertices, faces, and bodies in a "blocks world" scene, using the algorithm of Shirai (1975). We will assume that the scene is stored on an auxiliary file as a line drawing.

We will store the scene in a LISP array, using the array functions provided by our LISP system.

```
(ARRAY VIEW T '(1 . 80) '(1 . 80))
```

This declares a two dimensional array whose name is VIEW, and whose subscripts in both dimensions are between 1 and 80 inclusive. Each element is initially given the value NIL.

We refer to the element in the Rth row and Cth column of our array as (VIEW R C), and store the value V in it by evaluating the form (STORE (VIEW R C) V). Since this storage function is messy, we will define our own.

```
(STORE-VIEW R C V)
```

Stores the value V in the Rth row, Cth column of the array VIEW.

```
(DEFPROP STORE-VIEW
 (LAMBDA (R C V) (STORE (VIEW R C) V))
 EXPR)
```

The first thing we will have to do is read the scene into our array.

(VIEW-IN FILE)

Reads a line drawing from the file FILE and stores it in the array VIEW. Also, it sets the global variable MAXC to the largest column number actually used and the global variable MAXR to the largest row number used.

```
(DEFPROP VIEW-IN
 (LAMBDA (FILE)
  (PROG    (CH R C)
           (EVAL (LIST 'INC (LIST 'INPUT 'DSK: FILE)))
           (SETQ MAXC 0)
           (SETQ R 1)
           (ERRSET (REPEAT (SETQ C 1)
                           (REPEAT
                            UNTIL (EQ (SETQ CH (TYI)) 13)
                                  (STORE-VIEW R C (INTERN (ASCII CH)))
                                  (SETQ C (ADD1 C)))
                           (TYI)
                           (COND
                            ((GREATERP C MAXC) (SETQ MAXC (SUB1 C))))
                           (SETQ R (ADD1 R)))
                   T)
           (SETQ MAXR (SUB1 R))
           (INC NIL T)))
EXPR)
```

The innermost loop reads and stores characters in a row of VIEW until an end-of-line character (ASCII 13) is read.

(PRIN-VIEW)

This prints the scene as stored in the array VIEW.

```
(DEFPROP PRIN-VIEW
 (LAMBDA NIL
  (PROG (R C)
        (SETQ R 1)
        (REPEAT (SETQ C 1)
                (REPEAT
                 WHILE (VIEW R C)
                       (PRINC (VIEW R C))
```

```
        WHILE (LESSP C MAXC)
                (SETQ C (ADD1 C)))
            (PRIN3 <>)
        WHILE (LESSP R MAXR)
                (SETQ R (ADD1 R)))))
EXPR)
```

Note that any element that never had a character read into it is still NIL. The inner loop is stopped either by MAXC or by an element's being NIL, allowing for rows of different length.

Basic Functions for Points and Lines

We will represent a point of the picture as a dotted pair (R . C), which is more concise than (VIEW R C). We will represent a line as a list of points.

We will assume that the original drawing has an X at a point where a line occurs, and a blank where no line occurs. It will be the job of our program to find the lines and corners of the picture that represent the edges and vertices of the blocks of the pictured scene. To help us see what the program does, we will put a C in the array where the program identifies a corner, and an L where it identifies an interior point of a line. The following are basic functions for dealing with our points and lines.

(SET-VIEW PT V)

Stores the value V in the array element of the point PT.

```
(DEFPROP SET-VIEW
 (LAMBDA (PT V) (STORE (VIEW (CAR PT) (CDR PT)) V))
EXPR)
```

(POINT PT)

Returns the character stored in the array at the point PT.

```
(DEFPROP POINT
 (LAMBDA (PT) (VIEW (CAR PT) (CDR PT)))
EXPR)
```

(POINT? R C)

Returns T if there is an actual point in the scene at the point (R . C).

```
(DEFPROP POINT?
 (LAMBDA (R C) (MEMBER (VIEW R C) '(X L C)))
EXPR)
```

A point of the original line drawing is marked with an X, one discovered by the program to be a corner is marked with a C, one discovered to be on a line is marked with an L.

```
(END1 LN)
```

Returns the point at the "near end" of the line LN.

```
(DEFPROP END1
 (LAMBDA (LN) (CAR LN))
EXPR)
```

```
(END2 LN)
```

Returns the point at the "far end" of the line.

```
(DEFPROP END2
 (LAMBDA (LN) (RAC LN))
EXPR)
```

```
(SLOPE LN)
```

Returns the slope of the line LN as a dotted pair (DR . DC). Note that our rows increase going down and our columns increase to the right.

```
                    DC = 5
        end1    X ‾ ‾ ‾ ‾ ‾ ⌐
                  X        |
        LN        X        |   DR = 5
                    X      |
                     X     |
                      X    end2
```

```
(DEFPROP SLOPE
 (LAMBDA (LN) (DSLOPE (END1 LN) (END2 LN)))
EXPR)
```

```
(DSLOPE P1 P2)
```

Returns the slope of the line joining P1 as the "near" end and P2 as the "far" end.

```
(DEFPROP DSLOPE
 (LAMBDA (P1 P2)
  (CONS   (DIFFERENCE (CAR P2) (CAR P1))
          (DIFFERENCE (CDR P2) (CDR P1))))
EXPR)
```

===

(MARK-ENDS LN)

Marks the two ends of the line LN as corners of the scene, and returns LN.

```
(DEFPROP MARK-ENDS
 (LAMBDA (LN)
  (PROG NIL
        (SET-VIEW (END1 LN) 'C)
        (SET-VIEW (END2 LN) 'C)
        (RETURN LN)))
EXPR)
```

===

(MARK-LINE LN)

Marks all the points on the line LN, and returns LN.

```
(DEFPROP MARK-LINE
 (LAMBDA (LN)
  (PROG NIL
        (MAPC (FUNCTION
                (LAMBDA (P)
                 (COND
                  ((EQ (POINT P) 'X)
                   (SET-VIEW P 'L)))))
              LN)
        (MARK-ENDS LN)
        (RETURN LN)))
EXPR)
```

Note that only points presently marked X are changed to L, since there may be an end of another line on LN already marked C.

===

Finding the Contour

The first thing to do with the picture is to find the contour points on a connected group of bodies. We will do this by scanning each column from top to bottom starting with column 1 until we find a point (it will have an X in it). This will be a convex corner. Why? Then, starting with the neighbor up and to the right, at relative location

(–1 . 1), we will scan the immediate neighbors clockwise until we find another point. We will continue scanning clockwise around each point, always starting one position clockwise from the previous point, thus crawling clockwise around the connected group of bodies collecting contour points until we again arrive at the first point we found.

To help us in this circular search, we will make a list of the eight neighboring positions of a point going clockwise.

```
(SETQ SLOPES-1 '((–1 . 1) (0 . 1) (1 . 1) (1 . 0)
                 (1 . –1) (0 . –1) (–1 . –1) (–1 . 0)))
```

Actually, we could use a list exactly double this one, so that we could scan down it to find a starting point, then use the next eight elements.

```
(SETQ SLOPES-1 (APPEND SLOPES-1 SLOPES -1))
```

(FIND-CONTOUR)

Returns a list of contour points going clockwise around the first connected group of bodies found in the picture stored in VIEW. The first point will be marked as a corner, the rest as line points. The first point found will be both the first and the last element of the list of points.

```
(DEFPROP FIND-CONTOUR
 (LAMBDA NIL
  (PROG (C-POINTS PT SLP)
        (COND
          ((NULL (SETQ PT (LOC-CORNER)))
           (RETURN '(CANT FIND CORNER))))
        (SET-VIEW PT 'C)
        (SETQ C-POINTS (LIST PT))
        (SETQ SLP '(–1 . 0))
        (REPEAT
           WHILE (SETQ PT (C-SEARCH (CAR PT) (CDR PT) SLP SLOPES-1))
                 (SETQ C-POINTS (CONS PT C-POINTS))
           UNTIL (EQ (POINT PT) 'C)
                 (SET-VIEW PT 'L)
                 (SETQ SLP (DSLOPE PT (CADR C-POINTS))))
        (RETURN (REVERSE C-POINTS))))
 EXPR)
```

(LOC-CORNER)

Scans VIEW down the columns from left to right until it finds an X and returns the point found.

```
(DEFPROP LOC-CORNER
 (LAMBDA NIL
  (PROG (R C)
        (SETQ C 1)
        (COND
          ((REPEAT (SETQ R 1)
              UNTIL (REPEAT
                        UNTIL (POINT? R C)
                        WHILE (LESSP R MAXR)
                            (SETQ R (ADD1 R)))
              WHILE (LESSP C MAXC)
                  (SETQ C (ADD1 C)))
          (RETURN (CONS R C))))))
EXPR)
```

```
(C-SEARCH THISR THISC SLOPE SLOPES)
```

Searches circularly around the point (THISR . THISC) using the list of relative positions SLOPES starting in the position after SLOPE until a picture point is found. The found point is returned.

```
(DEFPROP C-SEARCH
 (LAMBDA (THISR THISC SLOPE SLOPES)
  (PROG NIL
        (REPEAT
           UNTIL (EQUAL (CAR SLOPES) SLOPE)
                 (SETQ SLOPES (CDR SLOPES)))
        (COND
          ((REPEAT (SETQ SLOPES (CDR SLOPES))
             WHILE  (NOT (EQUAL (CAR SLOPES) SLOPE))
             UNTIL  (POINT? (PLUS THISR (CAAR SLOPES))
                            (PLUS THISC (CDAR SLOPES))))
          (RETURN
            (CONS (PLUS THISR (CAAR SLOPES))
                  (PLUS THISC (CDAR SLOPES)))))))))
EXPR)
```

Breaking a List of Points into Lines

The next thing to do is to divide the list of contour points into contour lines. As we consider the points, we ask "Is this point in the middle of the line we are working on, or is it near the corner where this line joins another?" Consider the angle between one end of a line, the point in question, and the nth point beyond that point.

The closer this angle is to 180 degrees, the more sure we are that we are in the middle of a line. The closer the angle is to 90 degrees, the more sure we are that we are at a corner. So let us calculate the absolute value of the tangent of the angle (a relatively easy calculation given the three points). The larger this number is (let us refer to it as the ABTAN), the more sure we are that we are at a corner. So we will do the following. First choose n, call it THRESHL.

```
(SETQ THRESHL 4)
```

Starting with the THRESHLth point past the first point of a line, we will compare the ABTAN with some threshhold value, THRESHA.

```
(SETQ THRESHA 0.51)
```

As long as we are below the threshhold, we will assume that we are still on a line. As soon as we get above the threshhold, we will assume that we are nearing a corner, and will expect the ABTAN to increase until the actual corner is reached and then decrease back to THRESHA. We will declare the point where this local maximum is reached to be the corner.

```
(LINES POINTS)
```

LINES takes the list of points POINTS, divides it into lines as discussed above, and returns the list of lines. It also marks the lines in the array VIEW.

```
(DEFPROP LINES
 (LAMBDA (POINTS)
  (COND   ((NULL POINTS) NIL)
          (T (CONS (MARK-ENDS (CAR (SETQ POINTS (LINE POINTS))))
                   (LINES (CDR POINTS))))))
EXPR)
```

```
(LINE POINTS)
```

LINE takes a list of points POINTS, finds the first line on it, and returns a list whose CAR is the line and whose CDR is the rest of the points. The first of those remaining points is END2 of the line and END1 of the next line.

```
(DEFPROP LINE
 (LAMBDA (POINTS)
  (PROG   (L END N)
          (SETQ END (CAR POINTS))
          (SETQ N THRESHL)
          (COND
            ((NOT
              (REPEAT
                WHILE POINTS
```

```
         UNTIL  (ZEROP N)
                (SETQ L (CONS (CAR POINTS) L))
                (SETQ POINTS (CDR POINTS))
                (SETQ N (SUB1 N))))
      (RETURN (LIST (REVERSE L))))
      ((REPEAT (SETQ L (CONS (CAR POINTS) L))
               (SETQ POINTS (CDR POINTS))
        UNTIL (LESSP (LENGTH POINTS) THRESHL)
        WHILE (GREATERP THRESHA
                        (ABTAN END (CAR L) (NTH THRESHL
                        POINTS))))
       (RETURN (LIST (APPEND (REVERSE L) POINTS))))
      ((REPEAT
          UNTIL (LESSP (LENGTH POINTS) THRESHL)
          WHILE (LESSP (ABTAN END (CAR L)(NTH THRESHL POINTS))
                       (ABTAN END
                              (CAR POINTS)
                              (NTH (ADD1 THRESHL) POINTS)))
               (SETQ L (CONS  (CAR POINTS) L))
               (SETQ POINTS (CDR POINTS)))
       (RETURN (LIST (APPEND (REVERSE L) POINTS))))
      (T (RETURN (CONS (REVERSE L) (CONS (CAR L) POINTS)))))))))
EXPR)
```

The three sections of this function are as follows:

1. Peel off the first THRESHL points.

2. Peel off points until ABTAN rises above THRESHA.

3. Peel off points until the actual corner is reached. Of course, if we run out of points before this happens, the rest of the points are on this line, and we just return a list of this one line.

```
(ABTAN P1 P2 P3)
```

Returns the absolute value of the tangent of the angle P1, P2, P3.

```
(DEFPROP ABTAN
(LAMBDA (P1 P2 P3) (ABS (TAN (DSLOPE P1 P2) (DSLOPE P2 P3))))
EXPR)
```

```
(TAN SL1 SL2)
```

Returns the tangent of the angle between two lines whose slopes are SL1 and SL2.

```
(DEFPROP TAN
  (LAMBDA (SL1 SL2)
    (QUOTIENT (FLOAT
                (DIFFERENCE  (TIMES (CDR SL1) (CAR SL2))
                             (TIMES  (CDR SL2) (CAR SL1)))))
              (MAX (PLUS (TIMES (CDR SL1) (CDR SL2))
                         (TIMES (CAR SL1) (CAR SL2)))
                   1.0E-5)))
EXPR)
```

Extending Lines That Meet at a Concave Vertex

The next thing to do is to try to extend lines that meet at a concave vertex. Presumably, concave vertices are caused by one block's obscuring part of another. The extended line should be a boundary line of the obscuring block. The two tasks we need to do are (a) recognize whether a corner is concave; (b) follow and extend a line.

Consider two successive lines in our list of contour lines:

```
                          /
                         /
                        /          LLC  (R3 . C3)
                       /    LLL
          (R2 . C2)    CLLL
                         L              inside of figure
     outside of figure   L
                          L
          (R1 . C1)     C
```

Now translate both lines so that they each start at the origin.

```
   (R2-R1 . C2-C1)      C
                        L
                L      LLC  (R3-R2 . C3-C2)
                L   LLL
        (0 . 0)      CLLL
```

Finally, rotate the lines so that the first one lines up on the x axis. It may be seen that the corner at (R2 . C2) is concave just in case $(C2 - C1)*(R3 - R2) - (C3 - C2)*(R2 - R1)$ is negative (remember, rows increase going down).

To follow and extend a line, we consider several cases. If the line lies along a single row or column, it is easy. Just follow that row or column until there are no more points. It may be that, due to turning a concave corner, the line lies along a row or column except for the first or last point. In that case, we will discard that point and extend the rest of the line. Finally, we have the case of following a slopey line, which may be tricky because of the low resolution of our array. We will add points to the line by trying each of three neighbors of the currently last point, starting in the one predicted by the slope of the line as indicated below, until we find no point in any of those places.

```
                    CLL
                    LLL
                         LL3 ◄ – – – third try
        second try – – ► 21 ◄ – – – first try
```

Then we turn the extended list of points over to LINE to find exactly where the line should stop.

(EXTEND-CONCAVE LNS)

Takes a list of lines, LNS, and tries to extend those lines that meet at a concave corner. Returns the (possibly) modified list of lines. Any lines that are changed are reMARKed in the array VIEW.

```
(DEFPROP EXTEND-CONCAVE
 (LAMBDA (LNS)
  (COND  ((NULL (CDR LNS)) LNS)
         ((CONCAVE? (SLOPE (CAR LNS)) (SLOPE (CADR LNS)))
          (CONS (EXTEND (CAR LNS))
                (EXTEND-CONCAVE
                 (CONS
                  (REVERSE (EXTEND (REVERSE (CADR LNS))))
                  (CDDR LNS)))))
         (T (CONS  (CAR LNS) (EXTEND-CONCAVE (CDR LNS))))))
EXPR)
```

(CONCAVE? SL1 SL2)

Returns T if the corner between two lines, the first of slope SL1 and the second of slope SL2, is concave, NIL otherwise.

```
(DEFPROP CONCAVE?
 (LAMBDA (SL1 SL2)
  (MINUSP
    (DIFFERENCE (TIMES (CDR SL1) (CAR SL2))
                (TIMES (CDR SL2) (CAR SL1)))))
EXPR)
```

(EXTEND LN)

Tries to extend the line LN from its second end, and returns the (possibly) extended and reMARKed line.

```
(DEFPROP EXTEND
 (LAMBDA (LN) (MARK-LINE (FOLLOW (UNMARK-ENDS LN))))
EXPR)
```

(UNMARK-ENDS LN)

UnMARKs both ends of the line LN in the array VIEW.

```
(DEFPROP UNMARK-ENDS
 (LAMBDA (LN)
  (PROG NIL
        (SET-VIEW (END1 LN 'L)
        (SET-VIEW (END2 LN) 'L)
        (RETURN LN)))
EXPR)
```

(FOLLOW LN)

Returns the line, LN, extended if possible.

```
(DEFPROP FOLLOW
 (LAMBDA (LN)
  (OR  (FOLLOW-R LN)
       (FOLLOW-C LN)
       (FOLLOW-R (CDR LN))
       (FOLLOW-C (CDR LN))
       (FOLLOW-R (RDC LN))
       (FOLLOW-C (RDC LN))
       (FOLLOW-S LN)))
EXPR)
```

(FOLLOW-R LN)

Tries to extend the line LN along a row, and returns the (possibly) extended line.

```
(DEFPROP FOLLOW-R
 (LAMBDA (LN)
  (COND   ((STRAIGHT-R LN)
```

```
        (APPEND LN (FOLLOW1 (END2 LN) 0 (SIGN (CDR (SLOPE LN)))))))
        (T NIL)))
EXPR)
```

(FOLLOW-C LN)

Tries to extend the line LN along a column, and returns the (possibly) extended line.

```
(DEFPROP FOLLOW-C
 (LAMBDA (LN)
  (COND   ((STRAIGHT-C LN)
            (APPEND LN (FOLLOW1 (END2 LN) (SIGN (CAR (SLOPE LN))) 0)))
          (T NIL)))
EXPR)
```

(STRAIGHT-R LN)

Returns T if the line LN lies straight along a row, NIL otherwise.

```
(DEFPROP STRAIGHT-R
 (LAMBDA (LN)
  (REPEAT
    UNTIL   (NULL (CDR LN))
    WHILE   (EQ (CAAR LN) (CAADR LN))
            (SETQ LN (CDR LN))))
EXPR)
```

(STRAIGHT-C LN)

Returns T if the line LN lies straight along a column, NIL otherwise.

```
(DEFPROP STRAIGHT-C
 (LAMBDA (LN)
  (REPEAT
    UNTIL (NULL (CDR LN))
    WHILE (EQ (CDAR LN) (CDADR LN))
          (SETQ LN (CDR LN))))
EXPR)
```

(SIGN X)

Returns the sign of the number X.

```
(DEFPROP SIGN
 (LAMBDA (X) (COND ((ZEROP X) 0) ((LESSP X 0) –1) (T 1)))
EXPR)
```

(FOLLOW1 PT DR DC)

Returns the list of points that can be found in VIEW starting at the point PT, and each DR rows and DC columns from the previous one. Only the points subsequent to PT are in the returned list.

```
(DEFPROP FOLLOW1
 (LAMBDA (PT DR DC)
  (FOLLOW2 (PLUS (CAR PT) DR) (PLUS (CDR PT) DC) DR DC))
EXPR)
```

(FOLLOW2 R C DR DC)

Returns the list of points that can be found in VIEW starting at the point (R . C), and each DR rows and DC columns from the previous one.

```
(DEFPROP FOLLOW2
 (LAMBDA (R C DR DC)
  (COND   ((POINT? R C)
           (CONS (CONS R C) (FOLLOW2 (PLUS R DR) (PLUS C DC) DR DC)))
          (T NIL)))
EXPR)
```

(FOLLOW-S LN)

Tries to extend the "slopey" line LN, and returns the (possibly) extended line.

```
(DEFPROP FOLLOW-S
 (LAMBDA (LN)
  (CAR
   (LINE
    (APPEND LN
            (FOLLOW-S1 (CAR (END2 LN))
                       (CDR (END2 LN))
                       (TRY-SLOPES (SLOPE LN) SLOPES- 1))))))
EXPR)
```

(TRY-SLOPES S1 SLOPES)

Returns a list of three neighbor positions, the one predicted by the slope S1, and the two on either side of that one in the list SLOPES.

```
(DEFPROP TRY-SLOPES
 (LAMBDA (S1 SLOPES)
  (PROG NIL
        (SETQ S1 (CONS (SIGN (CAR S1)) (SIGN (CDR S1))))
        (REPEAT
          UNTIL  (EQUAL (CADR SLOPES) S1)
                 (SETQ SLOPES (CDR SLOPES)))
        (RETURN (LIST (CADR SLOPES) (CAR SLOPES) (CADDR SLOPES)))))
EXPR)
```

(FOLLOW-S1 R C SLPS)

Returns the list of points found in VIEW starting at the point (R . C), with each one in one of the neighboring positions listed in SLPS relative to the previous one. Only the points subsequent to (R . C) are in the returned list.

```
(DEFPROP FOLLOW-S1
 (LAMBDA (R C SLPS)
  (PROG   (NR NC SLP)
          (SETQ SLP SLPS)
          (RETURN
            (COND
              ((REPEAT
                 WHILE SLP
                       (SETQ NR (PLUS R (CAAR SLP)))
                       (SETQ NC (PLUS C (CDAR SLP)))
                 UNTIL (POINT? NR NC)
                       (SETQ SLP (CDR SLP)))
                (CONS (CONS NR NC) (FOLLOW-S1 NR NC SLPS)))
              (T NIL)))))
EXPR)
```

Example

We will now show a run in which a scene is read in, its contour is located and broken into lines, and contour lines that meet in a concave vertex are extended. We will show the list of points or lines and the array after each step.

```
*(VIEW-IN '(SCENE . DAT))
NIL
```

```
*(PRIN-VIEW)
```

```
                    XXXXX
                  XX     XXXXXXX
                 XX           XXXXXXX                    XXXXXXXXXXXXXXXXXXXXXXX
                XXX                    XXXX              XX                    XX
               XX                       XXX             X X                    XXX
              XX                        XX X            X XX                  XX X
             XXX                        XX X            X  XX                X   X
           XX                          XX  X            X   XX              XX   X
          XX                          XX   X            X    XX            XX    X
        XX                           XX    X            X     XX          XX     X
       XXXXX                        XX     X            X      XX        XX      X
       X    XXXX                   XX      X            X       XX      XX       X
       X       XXXXX              XX       X            X        XX    XX        X
       X           XXXX          XX        X            X         XX XX          X
       X             XXXX   XX              X           X          XXX           X
       X               XXXXX               XXXXXXXXXXXXXXXX         X            X
       X                  X               XX                       X            X
       X                  X              XX                       XX            X
       X                  X             XX                        XX            X
       X                  X            XX                        XXX            X
       X                  X           XX                        X X             X
       XXX                X          XX                        XX X             X
        XXXXX             X        XXX                        X   X             XX
       XX    XXXX         X  XX                              XX   X              XX
       X        XXXX      X XX                               X    X               XX
       X           XXXXX  XXX                               X     X                XX
       XX             XXXX XX                              XX     X     X           X
        X               XXX                               X      XX    X    XX
       XX                                                 XX     XXX  X  XX
        X                                                 X       X XX X XX
       XX                                                 XX      X  XXXXX
        X                                                 X       XX   XXX
        X                                                 X        X    X
       XX                                                 XX      XX
        X                                                 X       X
       XX                                                 XX      XX
        X                                                 X        X
       XX                                                 XX       XX
       XXXXXXXXXXXXXXXXXXXXXXXXXXXXXXXXXXXXXXXXXXXXXXXXXX   X        X
       X                                                  X        X X
       X                                                  X        XX
       X                                                  X        X
       X                                                  X       XX
       X                                                  X       X
       X                                                  X       X XX
       X                                                  X       X X
       X                                                  X       XX
       X                                                  XXX
       X                                                  XX
       XXXXXXXXXXXXXXXXXXXXXXXXXXXXXXXXXXXXXXXXXXXXXXXXXXXXXX
NIL
```

```
*(SETQ PTS (FIND-CONTOUR))

((39 . 2) (38 . 3) (37 . 3) (36 . 4) (35 . 4) (34 . 5) (33 . 5) (32 . 5) (31 . 6) (30 . 6) (29 .
  7) (28 . 7) (27 . 8) (26 . 8) (25 . 8) (24 . 9) (23 . 8) (22 . 8) (21 . 8) (20 . 8) (19 . 8)
(18 . 8) (17 . 8) (16 . 8) (15 . 8) (14 . 8) (13 . 8) (12 . 8) (11 . 8) (10 . 9) (9 . 10) (9 .
  11) (8 . 12) (7 . 13) (6 . 14) (5 . 15) (5 . 16) (4 . 17) (3 . 18) (2 . 19) (2 . 20) (2 . 21)
(2 . 22) (2 . 23) (2 . 24) (3 . 25) (3 . 26) (3 . 27) (3 . 28) (3 . 29) (3 . 30) (3 . 31) (4 .
  32) (4 . 33) (4 . 34) (4 . 35) (4 . 36) (4 . 37) (4 . 38) (5 . 39) (5 . 40) (5 . 41) (6 . 41)
(7 . 41) (8 . 41) (9 . 41) (10 . 41) (11 . 41) (12 . 41) (13 . 41) (14 . 41) (15 . 41) (16 .
41) (17 . 42) (17 . 43) (17 . 44) (17 . 45) (17 . 46) (17 . 47) (17 . 48) (17 . 49) (16 .
50) (15 . 50) (14 . 50) (13 . 50) (12 . 50) (11 . 50) (10 . 50) (9 . 50) (8 . 50) (7 . 50)
(6 . 50) (5 . 50) (4 . 50) (4 . 51) (4 . 52) (4 . 53) (4 . 54) (4 . 55) (4 . 56) (4 . 57) (4 .
  58) (4 . 59) (4 . 60) (4 . 61) (4 . 62) (4 . 63) (4 . 64) (4 . 65) (4 . 66) (4 . 67) (4 . 68)
(4 . 69) (4 . 70) (4 . 71) (5 . 71) (6 . 71) (7 . 71) (8 . 71) (9 . 71) (10 . 71) (11 . 71)
(12 . 71) (13 . 71) (14 . 71) (15 . 71) (16 . 71) (17 . 71) (18 . 71) (19 . 71) (20 . 71)
(21 . 71) (22 . 71) (23 . 71) (24 . 70) (25 . 69) (26 . 68 ) (27 . 67) (28 . 66) (29 . 65)
(30 . 65) (31 . 64) (32 . 63) (33 . 62) (34 . 61) (33 . 60) (32 . 59) (31 . 58) (30 . 57)
(31 . 56) (32 . 56) (33 . 56) (34 . 55) (35 . 55) (36 . 54) (37 . 54) (38 . 53) (39 . 53)
(40 . 52) (41 . 52) (42 . 52) (43 . 51) (44 . 51) (45 . 50) (46 . 50) (47 . 49) (48 . 49)
(49 . 49) (50 . 48) (51 . 48) (51 . 47) (51 . 46) (51 . 45) (51 . 44) (51 . 43) (51 . 42)
(51 . 41) (51 . 40) (51 . 39) (51 . 38) (51 . 37) (51 . 36) (51 . 35) (51 . 34) (51 . 33)
(51 . 32) (51 . 31) (51 . 30) (51 . 29) (51 . 28) (51 . 27) (51 . 26) (51 . 25) (51 . 24)
(51 . 23) (51 . 22) (51 . 21) (51 . 20) (51 . 19) (51 . 18) (51 . 17) (51 . 16) (51 . 15)
(51 . 14) (51 . 13) (51 . 12) (51 . 11) (51 . 10) (51 . 9) (51 . 8) (51 . 7) (51 . 6) (51 .
  5) (51 . 4) (51 . 3) (51 . 2) (50 . 2) (49 . 2) (48 . 2) (47 . 2) (46 . 2) (45 . 2) (44 . 2)
(43 . 2) (42 . 2) (41 . 2) (40 . 2) (39 . 2))
```

```
*(PRIN-VIEW)
```

```
                        IIIIIL
                   LX        XIIIIILL
                    LX            XLIIILLI
                   ILX                XLLL                LX                    IIIIIIIIIIIIILLLILIIIIL
                  LX                    XXL               I X                      LX                 XI
                  IX                    XX L              I XX                     I                   XXL
                 LXX                    XX I              L  XX                    I                  XX L
              II                        XX L             I    XX                   L                 XX  L
             LX                        XX   I            L      XX                 L                XX   L
            IX                         XX    L           I        XX               L               XX    L
            IXXXXX                    XX     L           I          XX             L              XX     L
           L      XXXX               XX      L           I            XX   XX       L             XX      L
           I         XXXXX          XX       L           I              XX XX       L            XXX      L
           L            XXXX       XX        I           I                XXX        L            X       I
           L              XXXX    XX         L           L                 X         L            X       I
           L                IIIIX            L      XIIIIILLLXXXXXXX        X         I
           I                 X             XX                              X         X            I
           L                 X            XX                              XX         X            I
           I                 X           XX                               XX         X            I
           L                 X          XX                               XXX         X            I
           I                 X         XX                                 X X         X            I
          LXX                X        XX                                  XX X        X           XI
            IXXXXX           X      XXX                                    X X        X          XI
          LX      XXXX       X     XX                                      X X        X         XL
          I          XXXX    X XX                                         X X        X        XL
          I            XXXXX   XXX                                        X X        X       XL
          LX             XXXX XX                                          XX X       X      L
           L               XXX                                            X  XX      X    L
            LX                                                            XX    XIX  X  XL
             L                                                            X      I IX X XL
            IX                                                            XX       L  LXXXL
             L                                                            X          XI   IXL
             L                                                            X           L    L
            IX                                                            XX       XI
             L                                                            X         L
            LX                                                            XX       XI
             L                                                            X         L
            CX                                                            X        XL
          LXXXXXXXXXXXXXXXXXXXXXXXXXXXXXXXXXXXXXXXXXXXXXXXXXXXXXXX        X         L
          L                                                              X         L
          L                                                              X        XI
          L                                                              X         I
          L                                                              X        XI
          L                                                              X         L
          L                                                              X       XI
          L                                                              X        L
          L                                                              X        L
          I                                                              XXI
          L                                                              XL
          IIIILLLLLLLLLLLLLLLLLLLLLILLILLLLLLLLLLLLLLIIIIIIIILLLL
          NIL
```

```
*(SETQ LNS (LINES PTS))

(((39 . 2) (38 . 3) (37 . 3) (36 . 4) (35 . 4) (34 . 5) (33 . 5) (32 . 5) (31 . 6) (30 . 6) (29
 . 7) (28 . 7) (27 . 8) (26 . 8) (25 . 8) (24 . 9))
                                                ((24 . 9) (23 . 8) (22 . 8) (21 . 8) (20 .
8) (19 . 8) (18 . 8) (17 . 8) (16 . 8) (15 . 8) (14 . 8) (13 . 8) (12 . 8) (11 . 8))
                                                                              ((11 . 8)
(10 . 9) (9 . 10) (9 . 11) (8 . 12) (7 . 13) (6 . 14) (5 . 15) (5 . 16) (4 . 17) (3 . 18) (2 .
 19))
        ((2 . 19) (2 . 20) (2 . 21) (2 . 22) (2 . 23) (2 . 24) (3 . 25) (3 . 26) (3 . 27) (3 .
28) (3 . 29) (3 . 30) (3 . 31) (4 . 32) (4 . 33) (4 . 34) (4 . 35) (4 . 36) (4 . 37) (4 . 38)
(5 . 39) (5 . 40) (5 . 41))
                        ((5 . 41) (6 . 41) (7 . 41) (8 . 41) (9 . 41) (10 . 41) (11 . 41)
(12 . 41) (13 . 41) (14 . 41) (15 . 41) (16 . 41) (17 . 42))
                                                ((17 . 42) (17 . 43) (17 . 44)
(17 . 45) (17 . 46) (17 . 47) (17 . 48) (17 . 49) (16 . 50))
                                                ((16 . 50) (15 . 50) (14 . 50)
(13 . 50) (12 . 50) (11 . 50) (10 . 50) (9 . 50) (8 . 50) (7 . 50) (6 . 50) (5 . 50) (4 .
 50))
      ((4 . 50) (4 . 51) (4 . 52) (4 . 53) (4 . 54) (4 . 55) (4 . 56) (4 . 57) (4 . 58) (4 .
59) (4 . 60) (4 . 61) (4 . 62) (4 . 63) (4 . 64) (4 . 65) (4 . 66) (4 . 67) (4 . 68) (4 . 69)
(4 . 70) (4 . 71))
                  ((4 . 71) (5 . 71) (6 . 71) (7 . 71) (8 . 71) (9 . 71) (10 . 71) (11 . 71)
(12 . 71) (13 . 71) (14 . 71) (15 . 71) (16 . 71) (17 . 71) (18 . 71) (19 . 71) (20 . 71)
(21 . 71) (22 . 71) (23 . 71))
                        ((23 . 71) (24 . 70) (25 . 69) (26 . 68) (27 . 67) (28 . 66)
(29 . 65) (30 . 65) (31 . 64) (32 . 63) (33 . 62) (34 . 61))
                                                ((34 . 61) (33 . 60) (32 . 59)
(31 . 58) (30 . 57))
                    ((30 . 57) (31 . 56) (32 . 56) (33 . 56) (34 . 55) (35 . 55) (36 . 54)
(37 . 54) (38 . 53) (39 . 53) (40 . 52) (41 . 52) (42 . 52) (43 . 51) (44 . 51) (45 . 50)
(46 . 50) (47 . 49) (48 . 49) (49 . 49) (50 . 48) (51 . 48))
                                                ((51 . 48) (51 . 47) (51 . 46)
(51 . 45) (51 . 44) (51 . 43) (51 . 42) (51 . 41) (51 . 40) (51 . 39) (51 . 38) (51 . 37)
(51 . 36) (51 . 35) (51 . 34) (51 . 33) (51 . 32) (51 . 31) (51 . 30) (51 . 29) (51 . 28)
(51 . 27) (51 . 26) (51 . 25) (51 . 24) (51 . 23) (51 . 22) (51 . 21) (51 . 20) (51 . 19)
(51 . 18) (51 . 17) (51 . 16) (51 . 15) (51 . 14) (51 . 13) (51 . 12) (51 . 11) (51 . 10)
(51 . 9) (51 . 8) (51 . 7) (51 . 6) (51 . 5) (51 . 4) (51 . 3) (51 . 2))
                                                        ((51 . 2) (50 . 2) (49
 . 2) (48 . 2) (47 . 2) (46 . 2) (45 . 2) (44 . 2) (43 . 2) (42 . 2) (41 . 2) (40 . 2) (39 . 2)))
```

```
*(PRIN-VIEW)
```

```
                    CILIIL
                  LX      XIIIILLI
                 LX                   XLLILLLI                    CIILIIIIIIILLLLILLLIILLLC
                LLX                        XLLC                  LX                        XL
               LX                          XXI                   L X                       XXL
              IX                           XX L                  L XX                     XX L
             LXX                           XX  L                 I   XX                   XX  L
            LL                             XX   L                I     XX                X   L
           IX                              XX    L               L       XX                XX   L
          CX                               XX     L              L         XX             XX     L
         LXXXXX                           XX       I             L           XX          XX       L
         I     XXXX                       XX        L            I             XX      XX          L
         L        XXXXX                   XX         I           I               XX  XX            L
         I            XXXX    XX          I          L           I                 XXX              L
         L              XXXX   XX         I          C                              X              L
         L                XXXXX          XCLLLLLLLXXXXXXX                           X              L
         L                    X          XX                                          X              L
         I                    X           XX                                      X  X              L
         L                    X            XX                                    XX  X              I
         I                    X             XX                                   XX  X              I
         L                    X              XX                                 XXX  X              I
         L                    X               XX                               X X   X              I
         IXX                  X                XX                             XX X    X             XC
          CXXXXX              X       XXX                                     X  X    X            XI
         IX      XXXX         X     XX                                      XX X     X            XL
         L          XXXX      X    XX                                       X  X     X           XL
         L             XXXXX  XXX                                          X   X     X          XL
         LX              XXXX XX                                          XX   X     X         L
          L                  XXX                                          X    XX    X      L
          LX                                                            XX       XCX  X   XL
           L                                                            X      L LX X  XL
          IX                                                            XX     I  IXXXL
          L                                                             X         XI   LXL
          L                                                             X          L      C
          LX                                                           XX      XI
          L                                                            X        L
          LX                                                           XX      XI
          L                                                            X        L
          CX                                                           X       XI
         LXXXXXXXXXXXXXXXXXXXXXXXXXXXXXXXXXXXXXXXXXXXXXXXXXXX           L
         L                                                             X        L
         L                                                             X       XL
         L                                                             X        L
         L                                                             X       XI
         L                                                             X        L
         L                                                             X XL
         L                                                             X L
         L                                                             X L
         L                                                             XXL
         L                                                             XL
         CLLLLIIIIIIIIIIIIILILLIIIIIIILLLLLIIILLIILLLLLLLC
```

NIL

*(EXTEND-CONCAVE LNS)

(((39 . 2) (38 . 3) (37 . 3) (36 . 4) (35 . 4) (34 . 5) (33 . 5) (32 . 5) (31 . 6) (30 . 6) (29
. 7) (28 . 7) (27 . 8) (26 . 8) (25 . 8) (24 . 9) (23 . 10))
                                        ((23 . 8) (22 . 8) (21 . 8) (20
. 8) (19 . 8) (18 . 8) (17 . 8) (16 . 8) (15 . 8) (14 . 8) (13 . 8) (12 . 8) (11 . 8))
                                                ((11
. 8) (10 . 9) (9 . 10) (9 . 11) (8 . 12) (7 . 13) (6 . 14) (5 . 15) (5 . 16) (4 . 17) (3 . 18)
(2 . 19))
        ((2 . 19) (2 . 20) (2 . 21) (2 . 22) (2 . 23) (2 . 24) (3 . 25) (3 . 26) (3 . 27) (3
. 28) (3 . 29) (3 . 30) (3 . 31) (4 . 32) (4 . 33) (4 . 34) (4 . 35) (4 . 36) (4 . 37) (4 .
38) (5 . 39) (5 . 40) (5 . 41))
                ((5 . 41) (6 . 41) (7 . 41) (8 . 41) (9 . 41) (10 . 41) (11 .
41) (12 . 41) (13 . 41) (14 . 41) (15 . 41) (16 . 41) (17 . 41) (18 . 41))
                                        ((17 . 41) (17
. 42) (17 . 43) (17 . 44) (17 . 45) (17 . 46) (17 . 47) (17 . 48) (17 . 49) (17 . 50) (17
. 51) (17 . 52) (17 . 53) (17 . 54) (17 . 55) (17 . 56))
                                ((17 . 50) (16 . 50) (15 . 50) (14
. 50) (13 . 50) (12 . 50) (11 . 50) (10 . 50) (9 . 50) (8 . 50) (7 . 50) (6 . 50) (5 . 50)
(4 . 50))
                ((4 . 50) (4 . 51) (4 . 52) (4 . 53) (4 . 54) (4 . 55) (4 . 56) (4 . 57) (4
. 58) (4 . 59) (4 . 60) (4 . 61) (4 . 62) (4 . 63) (4 . 64) (4 . 65) (4 . 66) (4 . 67) (4 . 68)
(4 . 69) (4 . 70) (4 . 71))
                ((4 . 71) (5 . 71) (6 . 71) (7 . 71) (8 . 71) (9 . 71) (10 . 71)
(11 . 71) (12 . 71) (13 . 71) (14 . 71) (15 . 71) (16 . 71) (17 . 71) (18 . 71) (19 . 71)
(20 . 71) (21 . 71) (22 . 71) (23 . 71))
                ((23 . 71) (24 . 70) (25 . 69) (26 . 68) (27 . 67)
(28 . 66) (29 . 65) (30 . 65) (31 . 64) (32 . 63) (33 . 62) (34 . 61))
                        ((34 . 61) (33 . 60)
(32 . 59) (31 . 58) (30 . 57) (29 . 56))
                        ((29 . 57) (30 . 57) (31 . 56) (32 . 56) (33 . 56)
(34 . 55) (35 . 55) (36 . 54) (37 . 54) (38 . 53) (39 . 53) (40 . 52) (41 . 52) (42 . 52)
(43 . 51) (44 . 51) (45 . 50) (46 . 50) (47 . 49) (48 . 49) (49 . 49) (50 . 48) (51 . 48))

((51 . 48) (51 . 47) (51 . 46) (51 . 45) (51 . 44) (51 . 43) (51 . 42) (51 . 41) (51 . 40)
(51 . 39) (51 . 38) (51 . 37) (51 . 36) (51 . 35) (51 . 34) (51 . 33) (51 . 32) (51 . 31)
(51 . 30) (51 . 29) (51 . 28) (51 . 27) (51 . 26) (51 . 25) (51 . 24) (51 . 23) (51 . 22)
(51 . 21) (51 . 20) (51 . 19) (51 . 18) (51 . 17) (51 . 16) (51 . 15) (51 . 14) (51 . 13)
(51 . 12) (51 . 11) (51 . 10) (51 . 9) (51 . 8) (51 . 7) (51 . 6) (51 . 5) (51 . 4) (51 . 3)
(51 . 2))
        ((51 . 2) (50 . 2) (49 . 2) (48 . 2) (47 . 2) (46 . 2) (45 . 2) (44 . 2) (43 . 2) (42
. 2) (41 . 2) (40 . 2) (39 . 2)))

`*(PRIN-VIEW)`

```
                    CLLLLL
                 LX       XLLLLLLL
                  LX                XLLLLLLL                  CLLLLLLLLLLLLLLLLLLLLC
                   LLX                      XLLC              IX                     XL
                    LX                        XXL             L X                    XXL
                   LX                         XX I            L XX                  XX  L
                  LXX                         XX I            L   XX                X   L
                II                            XX   L          L    XX              XX   L
               LX                             XX   I          L     XX            XX    L
              CX                            XX     L          L      XX          XX     L
              LXXXXX                       XX      I          L       XX        XX      L
              I      XXXX                  XX      L          L        XX      XX       L
              L        XXXXX              XX       I          L         XX    XX        L
              I          XXXX            XX        L          L          XX XX          L
              L            XXXX        XX          I          L           XXX           L
              L              XXXXX                 CLLLLLLLLCILLLLC         X            L
              L                  X              XC                X        X            L
              L                  X             XX                 XX       X            L
              I                  X            XX                  XX       X            L
              L                  X           XX                   XXX      X            L
              L                  X          XX                    X X      X            L
              I                  X         XX                     XX X     X           XC
              CXC                X       XXX                      X  X     X         XL
               LXXXXX            X     XX                        XX   X    X        XL
               IX    XXXX        X    XX                         X    X    X       XL
               L       XXXX      X XX                            X    X    X      XL
               I         XXXXX    XXX                            X    X    X     XL
              LX              XXXX XX                           XX    X    X    L
               L                XXX                             X    CC    X   L
              LX                                               XX    XLX  X  XL
               L                                               X    L LX X XL
              IX                                               XX   L  LXXXL
               L                                               X    XL  LXL
               L                                               X    L    C
              LX                                              XX    XL
               L                                              X     L
              LX                                             XX    XI
               L                                             X     L
              CX                                             X    XI
              LXXXXXXXXXXXXXXXXXXXXXXXXXXXXXXXXXXXXXXXXXXXXX  L
              L                                              X     L
              L                                              X    XL
              L                                              X    L
              L                                              X   XI
              L                                              X   L
              L                                              X  XL
              L                                              X  L
              L                                              X  L
              L                                              XXL
              L                                              XL
              CLLLLLIIIIIIIIILLIILLLIILIIIILLLLLLIIIILLLIILLLLLLLLC
```

NIL

Projects

5.2.1   Extend the program of this section by the following:

1.   Starting with the ends of extended lines that are apparently disconnected, use circular search followed by line following to find boundary lines of blocks within the group and divide the group into several bodies.

2.   Use small circular searches to find interior lines within convex corners and separate each block into faces.

5.2.2   Instead of starting with a line drawing, start with an intensity array. Use a change in intensity instead of the presence of an X to identify a line point.

Chapter 6
Concept Formation

Readings: Feigenbaum, 1963
Hunt, 1975—Chapters 6, 7
Slagle, 1971—pp. 163-174
Uhr, 1973—Chapter 15
Winston, 1977—Chapter 2

The following is a reconstruction of Feigenbaum's EPAM (Elementary Perceiver and Memorizer). It illustrates the techniques of building up and using discrimination nets (also called decision trees). EPAM simulates both learning and forgetting due to the interference of later learning.

EPAM can use a different decision tree for each "modality" (graphemic spelling, phonemic spelling, vision, hearing, etc.). Given a stimulus of some modality, the appropriate tree is used to find a list of response cues. The cue of the response modality is used with the tree of that modality to find a response to the original stimulus.

Each discrimination net is a binary tree composed of two kinds of nodes. Each branch node contains a test, the results of which determines which subtree will be searched. Each leaf contains an image of the original item stored there and a list of cues, one for each response modality.

It is assumed that each item to be filtered down a decision tree is a linear list of parts. Each branch node, therefore, also contains an extractor to indicate which part is to be tested by the test. For an extractor, we will use an integer that can be used as an index into the item.

Defining the Data Structure

For branch nodes, we will use the datatype, TEST-NODE

```
(DATA TEST-NODE (TEST PART TRUE FALSE))
```

whose fields are

TEST   The test to be applied, a predicate function of one argument.
PART   The part of the item to be tested, an integer.
TRUE   A subtree for those items passing the test.
FALSE   A subtree for those items failing the test.

For leaf nodes, we will use the datatype, IMAGE-LIST

```
(DATA IMAGE-LIST (IMAGE CUE-LIST))
```

whose fields are

IMAGE   An image of the item stored here.
CUE-LIST   A list of cues and modalities of the form.

```
( . . . (MODEi . CUEi) . . . )
```

```
(TEST? NODE ITEM)
```

Returns T if the item ITEM passes the test stored in the test-node NODE. Otherwise, returns NIL. However, if the item does not contain the part to be tested because it is only a partial image of some item, TEST? will return T or NIL randomly with a probability of 0.5.

```
(DEFPROP TEST?
 (LAMBDA (NODE ITEM)
  (COND
   ((NTH (PART NODE) ITEM) ((TEST NODE) (NTH (PART NODE) ITEM)))
   (T (GREATERP (RANDOM 0 1) 0.5)))))
EXPR)
```

```
(RANDOM MIN MAX)
```

Returns a pseudorandom number between MIN and MAX.

```
(DEFPROP RANDOM
 (LAMBDA (MIN MAX)
  (PROG2
   (COND ((GET 'RANDOM 'X)
          (PUT 'RANDOM
               'X
               (REMAINDER (PLUS (TIMES A (GET 'RANDOM 'X)) C) M)))
         (T (PUT 'RANDOM 'X (REMAINDER (TIME) M))))
   (PLUS  (QUOTIENT (TIMES (ADD1 (DIFFERENCE MAX MIN))
                           (GET 'RANDOM 'X))
                    M)
          MIN)))
EXPR)
```

This function uses the linear congruential method to generate pseudorandom numbers X_n, $0 \leqslant X_n < M$, according to the formula $X_n = (A*X_{n-1} + C) \bmod M$ and then returns the number MIN + ((MAX − MIN + 1) * X_n) / M which will be between MIN and MAX, inclusive. It is left to the reader to choose A, C, and M according to the available computer and language implementation. Chapter 3.2 of Knuth (1969) may be consulted for suggestions.

(CUE IMG-CUE MODE)

Returns the cue stored in the IMAGE-LIST, IMG-CUE, for the modality MODE. If such a cue is not present, CUE returns NIL.

```
(DEFPROP CUE
 (LAMBDA (IMG-CUE MODE)
  (CDR
   (SASSOC MODE
           (CUE-LIST IMG-CUE)
           (FUNCTION (LAMBDA NIL (CONS NIL NIL))))))
EXPR)
```

(TREE MODE)

Returns the decision tree for the modality, MODE.

```
(DEFPROP TREE
 (LAMBDA (MODE) (EVAL MODE))
EXPR)
```

Functions for Interacting with the User

(EPAM)

The main program. It first requests the stimulus and response modalities and then goes into a loop in which it requests a stimulus, prints a response, requests feedback, and learns if necessary. When the stimulus is just the character #, the loop terminates and the mode decision tree(s) are printed for our study.

```
(DEFPROP EPAM
 (LAMBDA NIL
  (PROG   (S-MODE R-MODE S R F)
          (PRIN3 WHAT IS THE STIMULUS MODE?)
          (SETQ S-MODE (READ))
          (PRIN3 WHAT IS THE RESPONSE MODE?)
          (SETQ R-MODE (READ))
```

```
      (PRIN3 <>WHEN ASKED FOR A STIMULUS/,
                YOU MAY TYPE # TO TERMINATE THE RUN/. <>)
      (REPEAT (PRIN3 STIMULUS:)
        UNTIL  (EQ (SETQ S (READ)) '#)
                (PRIN3 RESPONSE:
                        *(OR (SETQ R (RESPOND S S-MODE R-MODE))
                            BLANK)
                        <>
                        FEEDBACK:)
              (COND
               ((NOT (EQUAL R (SETQ F (READ))))
                (LEARN S S-MODE F R-MODE))))
      (DISPLAY S-MODE R-MODE)))
EXPR)
```

We assume that the variable BLANK is bound to the atom whose print name is one blank.

(DISPLAY SM RM)

Prints the trees for the modalities SM and RM in a readable format. If RM and SM are the same, the tree is printed only once.

```
(DEFPROP DISPLAY
 (LAMBDA (SM RM)
  (PROG NIL
      (PRIN3 <>THE TREE FOR THE *SM MODE IS: <>)
      (SPRINT (EVAL SM) 1 1)
      (COND
        ((NOT (EQ SM RM)) (PRIN3 <>THE TREE FOR THE *RM MODE IS:
                        <>)
                        (SPRINT (EVAL RM) 1 1)))))
EXPR)
```

Functions for Finding a Response

(RESPOND S S-MODE R-MODE)

Returns the IMAGE in the mode, R-MODE, of the learned response to the stimulus, S, which is in the modality S-MODE. Returns NIL if no such IMAGE can be found.

```
(DEFPROP RESPOND
 (LAMBDA (S S-MODE R-MODE)
  (RESPOND1
```

```
(DISCRIMINATE (CUE (DISCRIMINATE S (TREE S-MODE)) R-MODE)
            (TREE R-MODE))))
EXPR)
```

```
(RESPOND1 IMG-CUE)
```

If IMG-CUE is non-null, it is an IMAGE-LIST, and its IMAGE is returned. Otherwise, NIL is returned.

```
(DEFPROP RESPOND1
 (LAMBDA (IMG-CUE) (COND (IMG-CUE (IMAGE IMG-CUE)) (T NIL)))
EXPR)
```

```
(DISCRIMINATE ITEM TREE)
```

The item ITEM is discriminated down the decision tree, TREE, and the located leaf node is returned.

```
(DEFPROP DISCRIMINATE
 (LAMBDA (ITEM TREE)
  (COND   ((NULL TREE) NIL)
          ((EQ (CAR TREE) 'IMAGE-LIST) TREE)
          ((TEST? TREE ITEM) (DISCRIMINATE ITEM (TRUE TREE)))
          (T (DISCRIMINATE ITEM (FALSE TREE)))))
EXPR)
```

Functions for Learning

```
(LEARN S S-MODE R R-MODE)
```

The response R, in the modality, R-MODE, is learned as a response to the stimulus, S, which is in the modality S-MODE.

```
(DEFPROP LEARN
 (LAMBDA (S S-MODE R R-MODE)
  (PROG NIL
          (SET S-MODE (D-LEARN S (TREE S-MODE) (START-IMAGE S)))
          (SET R-MODE (D-LEARN R (TREE R-MODE) R))
          (SET S-MODE
               (STORE-CUE S
                       (TREE S-MODE)
                       (CONS R-MODE
```

```
                                        (FIND-CUE R
                                               (TREE R-MODE)
                                               (START-IMAGE R)))))))

EXPR)
```

```
(START-IMAGE L)
```

Returns an image of the item, L, which is a list of the same length as L, but with all parts NIL except for the most noticeable part which is the same as L.

```
(DEFPROP START-IMAGE
  (LAMBDA (L)
    (MAKENTH   (CAR NOTICE-LIST)
               (MAPCAR (FUNCTION (LAMBDA (X) NIL)) L)
               (NTH (CAR NOTICE-LIST) L)))
EXPR)
```

```
(D-LEARN ITEM TREE IMG)
```

Will insert an IMAGE-LIST for the item ITEM in the decision tree TREE. The IMAGE of the IMAGE-LIST will be IMG updated to include all additional parts of ITEM needed to find the IMAGE-LIST in TREE as it now is.

```
(DEFPROP D-LEARN
  (LAMBDA (ITEM TREE IMG)
    (COND   ((NULL TREE) (IMAGE-LIST IMG NIL))
            ((EQ (CAR TREE) 'IMAGE-LIST)
             (COND ((EQUAL (IMAGE TREE) ITEM) TREE)
                   (T (MAKE-TEST-NODE TREE (IMAGE TREE) ITEM IMG))))
            ((TEST? TREE ITEM)
             (TRUE TREE
                   (D-LEARN ITEM
                            (TRUE TREE)
                            (MAKENTH (PART TREE)
                                     IMG
                                     (NTH (PART TREE) ITEM)))))
            (T  (FALSE TREE
                       (D-LEARN ITEM
                                (FALSE TREE)
                                (MAKENTH (PART TREE)
                                         IMG
                                         (NTH (PART TREE) ITEM)))))))
EXPR)
```

(MAKE-TEST-NODE ITLO ITMO ITMN IMG)

Creates a new TEST-NODE to distinguish between ITMO, which is the IMAGE of the IMAGE-LIST, ITLO, and the item ITMN, whose image is IMG. Returns a tree whose root is the new TEST-NODE, and whose leaves are ITLO and a new IMAGE-LIST whose IMAGE is IMG.

```
(DEFPROP MAKE-TEST-NODE
 (LAMBDA (ITLO ITMO ITMN IMG)
  (M-T-N-1 ITLO ITMO ITMN IMG (FIND-PART ITMO ITMN NOTICE-LIST)))
EXPR)
```

(M-T-N-1 ITLO ITMO ITMN IMG PRT)

Creates a new TEST-NODE to distinguish between ITMO, which is the IMAGE of the IMAGE-LIST ITLO, and the item ITEM, whose image is IMG. The PART of the new TEST-NODE will be PRT, which is a part at which ITMO and ITMN differ. Returns a tree whose root is the new TEST-NODE, and whose leaves are ITLO and a new IMAGE-LIST whose IMAGE is IMG.

```
(DEFPROP M-T-N-1
 (LAMBDA (ITLO ITMO ITMN IMG PRT)
  (M-T-N-2 ITLO
           (IMAGE-LIST (MAKENTH PRT IMG (NTH PRT ITMN)) NIL)
           PRT
           (FIND-TEST (NTH PRT ITMO) (NTH PRT ITMN) TEST-LIST)))
EXPR)
```

(M-T-N-2 ITLO ITLN PRT TST)

Returns a new TEST-NODE whose TEST is TST, whose PART is PRT, and whose two subtrees are the IMAGE-LISTs ITLO and ITLN.

```
(DEFPROP M-T-N-2
 (LAMBDA (ITLO ITLN PRT TST)
  (COND  ((TST (NTH PRT (IMAGE ITLN))) (TEST-NODE TST PRT ITLN ITLO))
         (T (TEST-NODE TST PRT ITLO ITLN))))
EXPR)
```

(FIND-PART ITM1 ITM2 LPART)

Finds and returns the first part on the list of parts, LPART, which is a part at which ITM1 and ITM2 differ.

```
(DEFPROP FIND-PART
 (LAMBDA (ITM1 ITM2 LPART)
  (PROG2 (REPEAT
             WHILE  (EQUAL (NTH (CAR LPART) ITMO)
                              (NTH (CAR LPART) ITMN))
                  (SETQ LPART (CDR LPART)))
          (CAR LPART)))
EXPR)
```

(FIND-TEST FO FN LTEST)

Finds and returns the first test on the list of tests, LTEST, which gives different results for FO and FN. If there is no such test, an error message is printed, and the first test on the list TEST-LIST is returned.

```
(DEFPROP FIND-TEST
 (LAMBDA (FO FN LTEST)
  (COND
   (FO
    (COND
     ((REPEAT
       WHILE LTEST
       UNTIL (NOT (EQ ((CAR LTEST)FO) ((CAR LTEST)FN)))
            (SETQ LTEST (CDR LTEST)))
      (CAR LTEST))
     (T (PRIN3 <> : : : : : NO TEST CAN DISTINGUISH *FO FROM *FN <>)
        (CAR TEST-LIST))))
   (T (CAR LTEST))))
EXPR)
```

(FIND-CUE ITM TREE CUE)

CUE is a (possibly partial) image of the item ITM. FIND-CUE updates it with exactly those parts of the item ITM which are tested as ITM is filtered down to an IMAGE-LIST of the decision tree TREE.

```
(DEFPROP FIND-CUE
 (LAMBDA (ITM TREE CUE)
  (COND  ((EQ (CAR TREE) 'IMAGE-LIST) CUE)
         (T (FIND-CUE ITM
                 (COND
                   ((TEST? TREE ITM) (TRUE TREE))
                   (T (FALSE TREE)))
                 (MAKENTH (PART TREE)
```

```
                              CUE
                              (NTH (PART TREE) ITM))))))
EXPR)
```

```
(STORE-CUE ITM TREE CUE-PR)
```

Returns an updated version of the decision tree TREE, with CUE-PR added to the CUE-LIST of the IMAGE-LIST to which the item ITM is filtered.

```
(DEFPROP STORE-CUE
  (LAMBDA (ITM TREE CUE-PR)
    (COND
      ((EQ (CAR TREE) 'IMAGE-LIST)
       (CUE-LIST TREE (CONS CUE-PR (CUE-LIST TREE))))
      ((TEST? TREE ITM) (TRUE TREE (STORE-CUE ITM (TRUE TREE) CUE-PR)))
      (T (FALSE TREE (STORE-CUE ITM (FALSE TREE) CUE-PR)))))
EXPR)
```

Example

As an example, we will run a paired-associate task on nonsense syllables. We will use the same modality, LIT, for stimulus and response.

```
(SETQ LIT NIL)
```

We will set up the NOTICE-LIST to look at the first letter first, then the third letter, then the second letter.

```
(SETQ NOTICE-LIST '(1 3 2))
```

Finally, we establish a list of tests each of which accepts any of some set of letters. These tests represent the "features": contains a loop; has a horizontal line in the middle; has a diagonal line; has no straight line; has a horizontal line or curve at the bottom.

```
(SETQ TEST-LIST
      (QUOTE
        ((LAMBDA (X) (MEMBER X '(A B D O P Q R)))
         (LAMBDA (X) (MEMBER X '(A B E F G H P R)))
         (LAMBDA (X) (MEMBER X '(A K W X Y)))
         (LAMBDA (X) (MEMBER X '(C O S U)))
         (LAMBDA (X) (MEMBER X '(B C D E G I J L O Q S U Z)))))))
```

We now run the program.

```
(EPAM)
WHAT IS THE STIMULUS MODE? LIT
WHAT IS THE RESPONSE MODE? LIT
WHEN ASKED FOR A STIMULUS, YOU MAY TYPE # TO TERMINATE THE RUN.
STIMULUS:   (D A X)
RESPONSE:
FEEDBACK:  (J I R)
STIMULUS:   (P I B)
RESPONSE:  (J I R)
FEEDBACK:  (J U K)
STIMULUS:   (P I B)
RESPONSE:  (J U K)
FEEDBACK:  (J U K)
STIMULUS:   (D A X)
RESPONSE:  (J U K)
FEEDBACK:  (J I R)
STIMULUS:   (D A X)
RESPONSE:  (J I R)
FEEDBACK:  (J I R)
STIMULUS:   (P I B)
RESPONSE:  (J U K)
FEEDBACK:  (J U K)
STIMULUS:   #
THE TREE FOR THE LIT MODE IS:
(TEST-NODE (LAMBDA (X) (MEMBER X '(A B D O P Q R)))
            1
            (TEST-NODE (LAMBDA (X) (MEMBER X '(A B E F G H P R)))
                       1
                       (IMAGE-LIST (P NIL NIL) ((LIT J NIL K)))
                       (TEST-NODE (LAMBDA (X)
                                  (MEMBER X '(A B D O P Q R)))
                             3
                             (IMAGE-LIST (D NIL NIL)
                                   ((LIT J NIL NIL)))
                             (IMAGE-LIST (D NIL X)
                                   ((LIT J NIL R)))))
            (TEST-NODE (LAMBDA (X) (MEMBER X '(A B D O P Q R)))
                       3
                       (IMAGE-LIST (J I R) NIL)
                       (IMAGE-LIST (J U K) NIL)))
NIL
```

We will now run a "reading aloud" task using the same LIT mode for the stimuli, but a PHONetic mode for the responses.

(SETQ PHON NIL)

(EPAM)

WHAT IS THE STIMULUS MODE? LIT
WHAT IS THE RESPONSE MODE? PHON

WHEN ASKED FOR A STIMULUS, YOU MAY TYPE # TO TERMINATE THE RUN.
STIMULUS: (C A R)
RESPONSE:
FEEDBACK: (K AH R)
STIMULUS: (D O G)
RESPONSE: (K AH R)
FEEDBACK: (D AW G)
STIMULUS: (C A T)
RESPONSE: (K AH R)
FEEDBACK: (K A T)
STIMULUS: (B A L L)
RESPONSE: (K A T)
FEEDBACK: (B AW L)
STIMULUS: (D O G)
RESPONSE: (D AW G)
FEEDBACK: (D AW G)
STIMULUS: (B A L L)
RESPONSE: (B AW L)
FEEDBACK: (B AW L)
STIMULUS: (C A T)
RESPONSE: (K A T)
FEEDBACK: (K A T)
STIMULUS: (C A R)
RESPONSE: (K A T)
FEEDBACK: (K AH R)
STIMULUS: (D O G)
RESPONSE: (D AW G)
FEEDBACK: (D AW G)
STIMULUS: (C A T)
RESPONSE: (K A T)
FEEDBACK: (K A T)
STIMULUS: (B A L L)
RESPONSE: (B AW L)
FEEDBACK: (B AW L)
STIMULUS: (C A R)
RESPONSE: (K AH R)
FEEDBACK: (K AH R)
STIMULUS: #

THE TREE FOR THE LIT MODE IS:

```
(TEST-NODE (LAMBDA (X) (MEMBER X '(A B D O P Q R)))
          1
            (TEST-NODE (LAMBDA (X) (MEMBER X '(A B E F G H P R)))
                    1
                      (TEST-NODE (LAMBDA (X)
                              (MEMBER X '(B C D E G I J O Q S U Z)))
                              1
                              (IMAGE-LIST (B NIL NIL NIL)
                                      ((PHON B NIL NIL)))
                              (IMAGE-LIST (P NIL NIL)
                                      ((LIT J NIL K))))
                      (TEST-NODE (LAMBDA (X)
                              (MEMBER X '(A B D O P Q R)))
                              3
                              (IMAGE-LIST (D NIL NIL)
                                      ((LIT J NIL NIL)))
                              (TEST-NODE
                               (LAMBDA (X)
                                (MEMBER X '(A B E F G H P R)))
                               3
                               (IMAGE-LIST (D NIL G)
                                       ((PHON D NIL NIL)))
                               (IMAGE-LIST (D NIL X)
                                       ((LIT J NIL R))))))
            (TEST-NODE (LAMBDA (X) (MEMBER X '(A B D O P Q R)))
                    3
                    (TEST-NODE (LAMBDA (X)
                            (MEMBER X '(C O S U)))
                            1
                            (TEST-NODE
                             (LAMBDA (X)
                              (MEMBER X '(A B D O P Q R)))
                             2
                             (IMAGE-LIST (C A R)
                                     ((PHON K NIL R)))
                             (IMAGE-LIST (C NIL R)
                                     ((PHON K NIL NIL))))
                            (IMAGE-LIST (J I R) NIL))
                    (TEST-NODE (LAMBDA (X)
                            (MEMBER X '(C O S U)))
                            1
                            (IMAGE-LIST (C NIL T)
                                    ((PHON K NIL T)))
                            (IMAGE-LIST (J U K) NIL))))
```

THE TREE FOR THE PHON MODE IS:

```
(TEST-NODE (LAMBDA (X) (MEMBER X '(A B D O P Q R)))
            1
            (TEST-NODE (LAMBDA (X) (MEMBER X '(A B E F G H P R)))
                        1
                        (IMAGE-LIST (B AW L) NIL)
                        (IMAGE-LIST (D AW G) NIL))
            (TEST-NODE (LAMBDA (X) (MEMBER X '(A B D O P Q R)))
                        3
                        (IMAGE-LIST (K AH R) NIL)
                        (IMAGE-LIST (K A T) NIL)))
NIL
```

Projects

6.1 Two features mentioned in Feigenbaum (1963) are not in the code of this section: (a) when a new TEST-NODE is added, one or more extra TEST-NODEs are added giving one empty IMAGE-LIST per extra TEST-NODE (p. 303 ff.); (b) the extractor found by FIND-PART is promoted one position higher in NOTICE-LIST so EPAM can learn which parts are most important (p. 304). Add these two features to the code of this section and assess the difference they make.

6.2 Change the program to allow for a sequence of modalities, $M1, \ldots, Mk$. Accept a stimulus in mode $M1$. When an IMAGE-LIST in mode Mi ($i < k$) is found, use its cue for mode $Mi + 1$ in that tree, and finally respond in modality Mk. Training may be done in two modalities at a time.

6.3 Change the program so that each modality has its own NOTICE-LIST and TEST-LIST.

6.4 Explore EPAM as a concept formation program, where the parts of stimuli are different features such as color, size, or shape and the responses are class names.

6.5 See if EPAM can learn the concept "arch" after the manner of Winston, 1975b (see also Jackson, 1974, pp. 201-209 or Winston, 1977, Chap. 2). You may devise a different data structure than Winston's description graphs, but include the same information he has. Compare the tree that EPAM learns to the graph that Winston's program learns.

Chapter 7
Deductive
Question Answering

Readings: Hunt, 1975–Chapter XIV
                Jackson, 1974–Chapter 7
                Raphael, 1976–Chapter 6
                Winston, 1977–Chapter 7

This section contains a reconstruction of Raphael's SIR (Semantic Information Retrieval), which is described briefly in Raphael (1964), and in more detail in Raphael (1968). SIR was the first deductive question-answering program to use a general relational graph as a data base and so is one of the forerunners of the semantic networks used today. For our representation of relational graphs, we will use what Raphael called type-2 links rather than the type-3 links he used to allow for the "a hand has 5 fingers" example. In this method, if object A has relation R to object B, the relational graph has a directed arc labeled R going from a node labeled A to a node labeled B, and the implementation will put the property R on the property list of the atom A with a list containing the atom B as value.

To handle English input, SIR used the notion of a sentence frame. This is a pattern containing words and blanks. A sentence matches the pattern if it can be made from it by filling in the blanks with any sequences of words. In addition, each blank can have associated with it a predicate restricting the sequence of words that can be used to fill it. Such a pattern, together with a semantic interpretation, or "action," which tells the system what to do if the input sentence matches the pattern, forms a rule. SIR must be provided with a list of such rules and the definitions of the restricting predicates and of the semantic actions. The basic SIR procedure is to input a sentence, find the first rule whose pattern matches, and perform the action. A value is returned which SIR prints. SIR then processes the next sentence.

Functions for the Top Level of SIR

(SIR)

Gets and processes sentences until a sentence begins with the word "BYE," then returns "GOOD-BYE."

```
(DEFPROP SIR
 (LAMBDA NIL
  (PROG (S)
       (REPEAT (SETQ S (GET-SENTENCE))
         UNTIL  (EQ (CAR S) 'BYE)
               (PROCESS S))
       (RETURN 'GOOD-BYE)))
EXPR)
```

(GET-SENTENCE)

Reads in one sentence, which must end either with a "!" or a "?" and returns the sentence in a list.

```
(DEFPROP GET-SENTENCE
 (LAMBDA NIL
  (PROG (S)
       (REPEAT (SETQ S (CONS (READ) S))
         UNTIL  (MEMBER (CAR S) '(! ?)))
       (RETURN (REVERSE S))))
EXPR)
```

(PROCESS SENTENCE)

Processes the sentence SENTENCE according to the rules in the global list RULE-LIST.

```
(DEFPROP PROCESS
 (LAMBDA (SENTENCE)
  (PROCESS-1 SENTENCE RULE-LIST))
EXPR)
```

(PROCESS-1 SENTENCE RULES)

The first rule in the list RULES that is applicable to the sentence SENTENCE is applied, and its value is printed. If no rule is applicable, an error message is printed.

```
(DEFPROP PROCESS-1
 (LAMBDA (SENTENCE RULES)
  (PROG (RESP)
```

```
       (COND ((REPEAT
              WHILE RULES
              UNTIL (SETQ RESP APPLY-RULE (CAR RULES) SENTENCE))
              (SETQ RULES (CDR RULES)))
              (EVALQUOTE (FUNCTION PRIN3) RESP)
              (PRIN3 <>))
             (T (PRIN3 STATEMENT FORM NOT RECOGNIZED <> <>)))))
EXPR)
```

Defining the Syntax of Rules

The rules we will use are just like those Raphael used, except that we will let a pattern be an atom as well as a list. If a pattern is an atom, it will mean "the same as the previous rule." We do this to make the rules more perspicuous without paying too high a price in efficiency. For each set of our rules with the same pattern, Raphael used one rule, and used the test predicates and action functions to perform the division into several rules that we have done directly.

A rule has four parts:

1. A PATTERN, which is either a list or an atom. An atom is to be interpreted as ditto marks, i. e., the same pattern as the previous rule.

2. A list of VARIABLES appearing in the pattern. Each variable represents a blank in the pattern. If a sentence matches the pattern, each variable is bound to the sequence of words filling its blank.

3. A list of TESTS, one for each variable. Each test, applied to its variable, returns NIL if the test fails or some non-NIL value if it succeeds.

4. An ACTION to be carried out if the pattern matches and the variables pass the tests. An action is a list of the form (ACT SELECTOR1 ... SELECTORk), where ACT is a function of k arguments and SELECTORi is a function which, applied to the list of test results, gives the ith argument for ACT.

```
(DEFPROP PATTERN
 (LAMBDA (RULE) (CAR RULE))
EXPR)

(DEFPROP VARIABLES
 (LAMBDA (RULE) (CADR RULE))
EXPR)

(DEFPROP TESTS
 (LAMBDA (RULE) (CADDR RULE))
EXPR)
```

```
(DEFPROP ACTION
  (LAMBDA (RULE) (CADDDR RULE))
EXPR)
```

Functions for Interpreting Rules

(APPLY-RULE RULE INP)

Tries to apply the rule RULE to the input sentence INP. Returns NIL if the rule does not apply, otherwise, returns a message that depends on the rule.

```
(DEFPROP APPLY-RULE
  (LAMBDA (RULE INP)
    (COND  ((MATCH INP (PATTERN RULE) (VARIABLES RULE))
            (APPLY-RULE-1 (APPLY-TESTS (TESTS RULE)
                                       (EVLIS (VARIABLES RULE)))
                          (ACTION RULE)))
           (T NIL)))
EXPR)
```

(MATCH INP PAT VARS)

Tries to match the pattern PAT with the input sentence INP. VARS is a list of variables in the pattern. If the pattern matches, each variable is set to the substring which it matches in INP and MATCH returns T. Otherwise, MATCH returns NIL.

```
(DEFPROP MATCH
  (LAMBDA (INP PAT VARS)
    (COND  ((ATOM PAT) MATCH-FLAG)
           (T (INITIALIZE VARS) (SETQ MATCH-FLAG (MATCH1 INP PAT
              VARS)))))
EXPR)
```

The global variable MATCH-FLAG is set to the value that MATCH returns, so if PAT is an atom, MATCH returns the value of MATCH-FLAG. If this is T, the variables still have the values they had when the previous rule matched.

(INITIALIZE LVARS)

Initializes each variable in the list LVARS to the value NIL.

```
(DEFPROP INITIALIZE
 (LAMBDA (LVARS)
  (MAPC (FUNCTION (LAMBDA (VAR) (SET VAR NIL))) LVARS))
EXPR)
```

```
(MATCH1 INP PAT VARS)
```

Tries to match the pattern PAT to the input sentence INP, setting the variables in the list VARS to the substrings of INP which they match. Returns T if PAT matches INP. Otherwise, it returns NIL.

```
(DEFPROP MATCH1
 (LAMBDA (INP PAT VARS)
   (COND  ((NULL INP) (NULL PAT))
          ((NULL PAT) NIL)
          ((MEMBER (CAR PAT) VARS)
           (COND ((NULL (CDR PAT))
                  (SET (CAR PAT) (APPEND (EVAL (CAR PAT)) INP)))
                 ((EQ (CAR INP) (CADR PAT))
                  (MATCH1 (CDR INP) (CDDR PAT) VARS))
                 (T (SET (CAR PAT) (SNOC (EVAL (CAR PAT)) (CAR INP)))
                    (MATCH1 (CDR INP) PAT VARS))))
          ((EQ (CAR INP) (CAR PAT)) (MATCH1 (CDR INP) (CDR PAT) VARS))
          (T NIL)))
EXPR)
```

```
(APPLY-TESTS TESTS PHRASES)
```

Applies the ith function on the list TESTS to the ith S-expression on the list PHRASES, and returns a list of the results unless any of these results is NIL, in which case NIL is returned. NIL is also returned if the two lists are of different lengths or if PHRASES is an empty list.

```
(DEFPROP APPLY-TESTS
 (LAMBDA (TEST PHRASES)
  (PROG (L)
        (COND ((AND PHRASES
                    (REPEAT
                      WHILE TESTS
                            (SETQ L (CONS ((CAR TESTS) (CAR
                              PHRASES)) L))
                      WHILE (CAR L)
                            (SETQ TESTS (CDR TESTS))
                            (SETQ PHRASES (CDR PHRASES))
```

```
                        UNTIL (AND (NULL TESTS) (NULL PHRASES))))
             (RETURN (REVERSE L)))
             (T (RETURN NIL)))))
EXPR)
```

```
(APPLY-RULE-1 L ACT)
```

Applies the action ACT, which is a list of functions, to *L*, which is a list of values, and returns the result.

```
(DEFPROP APPLY-RULE-1
 (LAMBDA (L ACT)
   (COND (L (EVALQUOTE (CAR ACT) (RMAPCAR L (CDR ACT))))))
EXPR)
```

```
(RMAPCAR S LF)
```

Applies each function on the list LF to the S-expression S, and returns a list of the results.

```
(DEFPROP RMAPCAR
 (LAMBDA (S LF)
   (COND   ((NULL LF) NIL)
           (T (CONS ((CAR LF) S) (RMAPCAR S (CDR LF))))))
EXPR)
```

General Functions for Relational Graphs

```
(ADD X REL Y)
```

Inserts an arc labeled REL from node X to node Y unless such an arc already exists.

```
(DEFPROP ADD
 (LAMBDA (X REL Y)
   (COND   ((MEMBER Y (GET X REL)) NIL)
           (T (PUT X REL (CONS Y (GET X REL))))))
EXPR)
```

```
(PATH X "ARC-PATH" Y)
```

Returns T if a path of arcs described by ARC-PATH exists from node X to node Y. The syntax of ARC-PATH can be described as follows:

1. Any atom is a basic path element.
2. A basic path element followed by "*" or by "+" is a path element.
3. A list of path elements is an **ARC-PATH**.
4. An **ARC-PATH** is also a basic path element.

A basic path element followed by a "*" means zero or more occurrences of that basic path element. A basic path element followed by a "+" means one or more occurrences of that basic path element.

```
(DEFPROP PATH
 (LAMBDA (X-RELS-Y ALIST)
  (MEMBER  (EVAL (CADDR X-RELS-Y) ALIST)
           (PATH1 (LIST (EVAL (CAR X-RELS-Y) ALIST)) (CADR X-RELS-Y))))
FEXPR)
```

```
(PATH1 LN LR)
```

Returns all nodes reachable from any of the nodes in the list LN by following the ARC-PATH LR.

```
(DEFPROP PATH1
 (LAMBDA (LN LR)
  (PROG2
   (REPEAT
     WHILE LN
     WHILE LR
              (COND  ((AND (CDR LR) (MEMBER (CADR LR) '(* +)))
                      (SETQ LN (EXTENDM (CADR LR) LN (CAR LR)))
                      (SETQ LR (CDR LR)))
                     (T (SETQ LN (EXTEND LN (CAR LR)))))
             (SETQ LR (CDR LR)))
    LN))
EXPR)
```

```
(EXTENDM OP LN R)
```

Returns the list of nodes reachable from any of the nodes on the list LN by following the path element consisting of the basic path element R followed by OP, which is either "*" or "+".

```
(DEFPROP EXTENDM
 (LAMBDA (OP LN R)
  (PROG (ANS)
          (COND ((EQ OP '+) (SETQ LN (EXTEND LN R))))
          (SETQ ANS LN)
```

```
        (REPEAT
          WHILE LN
                (SETQ LN (COMPLEMENT (EXTEND LN R) ANS))
                (SETQ ANS (APPEND ANS LN)))
          (RETURN ANS)))
EXPR)
```

(EXTEND LN R)

Returns the list of nodes reachable from any of the nodes on the list LN by following one instance of the basic path element R.

```
(DEFPROP EXTEND
 (LAMBDA (LN R)
  (COND  ((NULL LN) NIL)
         ((NOT (ATOM R)) (PATH1 LN R))
         (T (UNION (GET (CAR LN) R) (EXTEND (CDR LN) R)))))
EXPR)
```

(COMPLEMENT S1 S2)

Returns a set consisting of all those elements of the set S1 that are not also elements of the set S2.

```
(DEFPROP COMPLEMENT
 (LAMBDA (S1 S2)
  (COND  ((NULL S1) NIL)
         ((MEMBER (CAR S1) S2) (COMPLEMENT (CDR S1) S2))
         (T (CONS (CAR S1) (COMPLEMENT (CDR S1) S2)))))
EXPR)
```

(UNION S1 S2)

Returns a set consisting of all those elements that are either in the set S1 or in the set S2.

```
(DEFPROP UNION
 (LAMBDA (S1 S2)
  (COND  ((NULL S1) S2)
         ((MEMBER (CAR S1) S2) (UNION (CDR S1) S2))
         (T (CONS (CAR S1) (UNION (CDR S1) S2)))))
EXPR)
```

Test Functions for the Syntax of English Noun Phrases

The division of noun phrases into unique, generic, and specific as defined below is taken from Raphael (1968). First we define two global lists, one of generic determiners, and one of specific (definite) determiners.

```
(SETQ G-DETS '(EACH EVERY ANY A AN))
(SETQ S-DETS '(THE))
```

(UNIQUE NP)

If NP is a list of a single word, it is presumed to be a unique noun phrase, and that word is returned. Otherwise NIL is returned.

```
(DEFPROP UNIQUE
 (LAMBDA (NP)
  (COND ((NULL (CDR NP)) (CAR NP))))
EXPR)
```

(GENERIC NP)

If NP is a list of words beginning with a G-DET, it is presumed to be a generic noun phrase, and the last word is returned. Otherwise, NIL is returned.

```
(DEFPROP GENERIC
 (LAMBDA (NP)
  (COND ((MEMBER (CAR NP)  G-DETS) (RAC NP))))
EXPR)
```

(SPECIFIC NP)

If NP is a list of words beginning with an S-DET, it is presumed to be a specific noun phrase, and the last word is returned. Otherwise, NIL is returned.

```
(DEFPROP SPECIFIC
 (LAMBDA (NP)
  (COND ((MEMBER (CAR NP) S-DETS) (RAC NP))))
EXPR)
```

(UNIQUE-GENERIC NPNP)

If NPNP is a unique noun phrase followed by a generic noun phrase, a list is returned containing the one word of the former and the last word of the latter. Otherwise, NIL is returned.

```
(DEFPROP UNIQUE-GENERIC
 (LAMBDA (NPNP)
  (APPLY-TESTS '(UNIQUE GENERIC) (SPLIT NPNP G-DETS)))
EXPR)
```

(SPECIFIC-GENERIC NPNP)

If NPNP is a specific noun phrase followed by a generic noun phrase, a list is returned containing the last word of each. Otherwise, NIL is returned.

```
(DEFPROP SPECIFIC-GENERIC
 (LAMBDA (NPNP)
  (APPLY-TESTS '(SPECIFIC GENERIC) (SPLIT NPNP G-DETS)))
EXPR)
```

(GENERIC-GENERIC NPNP)

If NPNP is a generic noun phrase followed by another generic noun phrase, a list is returned containing the last word of each of them. Otherwise, NIL is returned.

```
(DEFPROP GENERIC-GENERIC
 (LAMBDA (NPNP)
  (APPLY-TESTS '(GENERIC GENERIC) (SPLIT NPNP G-DETS)))
EXPR)
```

(SPLIT SNP LD)

SNP is a list consisting of one or more noun phrases, and LD is a list of initial words of noun phrases (determiners). SPLIT returns a list of sublists, the ith sublist being the ith noun phrase in SNP.

```
(DEFPROP SPLIT
 (LAMBDA (SNP LD)
  (SPLIT1 (CDR SNP) LD (LIST (CAR SNP)) NIL))
EXPR)
(DEFPROP SPLIT1
 (LAMBDA (SNP LD NP LNP)
```

```
(COND  ((NULL SNP) (REVERSE (CONS (REVERSE NP) LNP)))
       ((MEMBER (CAR SNP) LD)
        (SPLIT1 (CDR SNP)
               LD
               (LIST (CAR SNP))
               (CONS (REVERSE NP) LNP)))
       (T (SPLIT1 (CDR SNP) LD (CONS (CAR SNP) NP) LNP))))
EXPR)
```

Action Functions

We present action functions for set relations, equivalence relations, and ownership relations. Except for the function **EQUIV-COMPRESS** and its help function, the functions given here have exactly the same names, arguments, and actions as specified in Raphael (1968). They are, however, implemented in a different way.

Some Messages for Actions to Return

```
(SETQ UNDERSTAND '(I UNDERSTAND <>))
(SETQ YES '(YES <>))
(SETQ SOMETIMES '(SOMETIMES <>))
(SETQ INSUFFICIENT '(INSUFFICIENT INFORMATION <>))
(SETQ SILENCE '(**NIL))
```

Action Functions for Information about Sets

```
(SETR X Y)
```

Adds the information that X is a subset of Y.

```
(DEFPROP SETR
 (LAMBDA (X Y)
  (PROGN  (ADD X 'SUBSET Y)
          (ADD Y 'SUPERSET X)
          UNDERSTAND))
EXPR)
```

```
(SETRQ X Y)
```

Determines if X is a subset of Y.

```
(DEFPROP SETRQ
 (LAMBDA (X Y)
```

```
       (COND   ((PATH X (SUBSET *) Y) YES)
               ((PATH Y (SUBSET +) X) SOMETIMES)
               (T INSUFFICIENT)))
EXPR)
```

(SETRS X Y)

Adds the information that X is a member of the set Y.

```
(DEFPROP SETRS
 (LAMBDA (X Y)
  (PROGN  (ADD X 'MEMBER Y)
          (ADD Y 'ELEMENTS X)
          UNDERSTAND))
EXPR)
```

(SETRSQ X Y)

Determines if X is a member of the set Y.

```
(DEFPROP SETRSQ
 (LAMBDA (X Y)
  (COND   ((PATH X (EQUIV * MEMBER SUBSET *) Y) YES)
          (T INSUFFICIENT)))
EXPR)
```

(SETRS1 X Y)

Adds the information that the unique element of the set X is an element of the
set Y. Does nothing if X has more than one element.

```
(DEFPROP SETRS1
 (LAMBDA (X Y)
  (COND   ((SETQ X (SPECIFY X)) (SETRS X Y))
          (T SILENCE)))
EXPR)
```

(SPECIFY X)

If X has a unique element, it is returned. If X has no elements, one is created
and returned. If X has more than one element, a message is printed and NIL is returned.

```
(DEFPROP SPECIFY
 (LAMBDA (X)
  (SPECIFY1 (EQUIV-COMPRESS (GET X 'ELEMENTS)) X))
EXPR)

(DEFPROP SPECIFY1
 (LAMBDA (U X)
  (COND  ((NULL U) (SETRS (SETQ U (GENSYM)) X) (PRIN3 *U IS A *X <>) U)
         ((NULL (CDR U)) (CAR U))
         (T (PRIN3 WHICH *X / . / . *U <>) NIL)))
EXPR)
```

```
(EQUIV-COMPRESS LX)
```

LX is a list of which some elements may be equivalent to some others. A list is returned of the elements of LX without such redundant members.

```
(DEFPROP EQUIV-COMPRESS
 (LAMBDA (LX)
  (EQUIV-COMP1 LX NIL))
EXPR)

(DEFPROP EQUIV-COMP1
 (LAMBDA (LX LEX)
  (COND   ((NULL LX) NIL)
          ((MEMBER (CAR LX) LEX) (EQUIV-COMP1 (CDR LX) LEX))
          (T (CONS (CAR LX)
                  (EQUIV-COMP1 (CDR LX)
                               (APPEND (GET (CAR LX) 'EQUIV)
                                       LEX))))))
EXPR)
```

```
(SETRS1 Q X Y)
```

Determines if the unique element of the set X (if there is one) is a member of the set Y.

```
(DEFPROP SETRS1Q
 (LAMBDA (X Y)
  (COND   ((SETQ X (SPECIFY X)) (SETRSQ X Y))
          (T SILENCE)))
EXPR)
```

Action Functions for the Equivalence Relation

(EQUIV X Y)

     Adds the information that X is equivalent to Y.

```
(DEFPROP EQUIV
 (LAMBDA (X Y)
  (PROGN (ADD X 'EQUIV Y) (ADD Y 'EQUIV X) UNDERSTAND))
EXPR)
```

(EQUIV1 X Y)

     If there is a unique element of the set Y, adds the information that it is equivalent to X.

```
(DEFPROP EQUIV1
 (LAMBDA (X Y)
  (COND   ((SETQ Y (SPECIFY Y)) (EQUIV X Y))
          (T SILENCE)))
EXPR)
```

Action Functions about Ownership

(OWNR X Y)

     Adds the information that every member of the set Y owns a member of the set X.

```
(DEFPROP OWNR
 (LAMBDA (X Y)
  (PROGN (ADD X 'OWNED-BY Y)
         (ADD Y 'POSSESS-BY-EACH X)
         UNDERSTAND))
EXPR)
```

(OWNRQ X Y)

     Determines if every member of the set Y owns a member of the set X.

```
(DEFPROP OWNRQ
 (LAMBDA (X Y)
  (COND   ((EQ X Y) '(NO! THEY ARE THE SAME <>))
```

```
        ((PATH Y (SUBSET * POSSESS-BY-EACH) X) YES)
        (T INSUFFICIENT)))
EXPR)
```

```
(OWNRGU X Y)
```

Adds the information that Y owns a member of the set X.

```
(DEFPROP OWNRGU
 (LAMBDA (X Y)
  (PROGN  (ADD Y 'POSSESS X) (ADD X 'OWNED Y) UNDERSTAND))
EXPR)
```

```
(OWNRGUQ X Y)
```

Determines if Y owns a member of the set X.

```
(DEFPROP OWNRGUQ
 (LAMBDA (X Y)
  (COND  ((PATH Y (EQUIV * POSSESS SUBSET *) X) YES)
         ((PATH Y (EQUIV * MEMBER SUBSET * POSSESS-BY-EACH
         SUBSET *) X) YES)
         (T INSUFFICIENT)))
EXPR)
```

```
(OWNRSGQ X Y)
```

Determines if some member of the set Y owns the unique element of the set X
(if such exists).

```
(DEFPROP OWNRSGQ
 (LAMBDA (X Y)
  (COND  ((NOT (SPECIFY X)) SILENCE)
         ((PATH X (OWNED EQUIV * MEMBER SUBSET *) Y) YES)
         (T INSUFFICIENT)))
EXPR)
```

A Set of Rules Using the Above Functions

```
(SETQ RULE-LIST ' (
   ((IS X ?) (X) (UNIQUE-GENERIC) (SETRSQ CAAR CADAR))
```

```
( ————————————— (X) (SPECIFIC-GENERIC) (SETRS1Q CAAR CADAR))
( ————————————— (X) (GENERIC-GENERIC) (SETRQ CAAR CADAR))
((DOES X OWN Y?) — (X Y) (GENERIC GENERIC) (OWNRQ CADR CAR))
( ————————————— (X Y) (UNIQUE GENERIC) (OWNRGUQ CADR CAR))
( ————————————— (X Y) (GENERIC SPECIFIC) (OWNRSGQ CADR CAR))
((X IS Y !) ——————— (X Y) (UNIQUE GENERIC) (SETRS CAR CADR))
( ————————————— (X Y) (GENERIC GENERIC) (SETR CAR CADR))
( ————————————— (X Y) (SPECIFIC GENERIC) (SETRS1 CAR CADR))
( ————————————— (X Y) (UNIQUE UNIQUE) (EQUIV CAR CADR))
( ————————————— (X Y) (UNIQUE SPECIFIC) (EQUIV1 CAR CADR))
( ————————————— (X Y) (SPECIFIC UNIQUE) (EQUIV1 CADR CAR))
((X OWNS Y !) ——— (X Y) (GENERIC GENERIC) (OWNR CADR CAR))
( ————————————— (X Y) (UNIQUE GENERIC) (OWNRGU CADR CAR))
))
```

Example

The following example is a modified version of the example in Raphael (1968).

(SIR)

ANY FEM-LIBBER IS AN EXAMPLE OF A MODERN-PERSON !
I UNDERSTAND

EVERY MODERN-PERSON IS A PERSON !
I UNDERSTAND

IS A FEM-LIBBER A PERSON ?
YES

IS A PERSON A PERSON ?
YES

IS A PERSON A MODERN-PERSON ?
SOMETIMES

IS A CHAUVINIST-PIG A PERSON ?
INSUFFICIENT INFORMATION

CAREN IS A MODERN-PERSON !
I UNDERSTAND

IS CAREN A PERSON ?
YES

IS SCHNERTZ A PERSON ?
INSUFFICIENT INFORMATION

THE MAN IS A CHAUVINIST-PIG !
G0001 IS A MAN
I UNDERSTAND

EVERY CHAUVINIST-PIG IS AN OLD-FASHIONED-PERSON !
I UNDERSTAND

IS THE MAN AN OLD-FASHIONED-PERSON ?
YES

STU IS A MAN !
I UNDERSTAND

IS THE MAN AN OLD-FASHIONED-PERSON ?
WHICH MAN . . (STU G0001)

CHARLIE IS A FIREMAN !
I UNDERSTAND

STU IS CHARLIE !
I UNDERSTAND

IS STU A FIREMAN ?
YES

IS THE FIREMAN A MAN ?
YES

IS EVERY FIREMAN A MAN ?
INSUFFICIENT INFORMATION

JUDI IS A FIREMAN !
I UNDERSTAND

JUDITH IS A FIREMAN !
I UNDERSTAND

IS THE FIREMAN A MAN ?
WHICH FIREMAN . . (JUDITH JUDI CHARLIE)

JUDI IS JUDITH !
I UNDERSTAND

IS THE FIREMAN A MAN ?
WHICH FIREMAN . . (JUDITH CHARLIE)

EVERY FIREMAN OWNS A PAIR OF RED SUSPENDERS !
I UNDERSTAND

DOES A DOCTOR OWN A PAIR OF RED SUSPENDERS ?
INSUFFICIENT INFORMATION

DOES A COAT OWN A COAT ?
NO! THEY ARE THE SAME

A FIRECHIEF IS A FIREMAN !
I UNDERSTAND

DOES A FIRECHIEF OWN A PAIR OF SUSPENDERS ?
YES

```
JUDITH IS THE FIRECHIEF !
G0002 IS A FIRECHIEF
I UNDERSTAND

DOES JUDI OWN A PAIR OF SUSPENDERS ?
YES

STU OWNS A CAT !
I UNDERSTAND

THE CAT IS SCHNERTZ !
G0003 IS A CAT
I UNDERSTAND

DOES A FIREMAN OWN THE CAT ?
YES

WHAT IS THE MEANING OF LIFE ?
STATEMENT FORM NOT RECOGNIZED

BYE !
GOOD-BYE
```

Projects

7.1   Provide this version of SIR with rules and action functions so that it handles additional relations, for example: part-whole, spatial (left, right, front, back, above, below), geographic (north, south, east, west, geographic containment, political containment).

7.2   Add the capability of dealing with an ambiguous word such as "has" meaning "has as parts" or "owns." See Raphael (1968, pp. 85-89).

7.3   Analyze the limitations of the sentence frame approach to parsing as presented in this section. Implement a better parser.

7.4   Add the ability to input sentences of the form

> **DEFINE MEMBER AS (EQUIV * MEMBER SUBSET *) !**

and to use such information during question-answering so that new relations can be defined by the user. Make this more useful by extending the syntax of ARC-PATHs to include conjunctions and disjunctions of ARC-PATHs.

7.5   Implement a question-answering system that can deal with sentences such as, "The mother of the father of Bill's wife is the wife of Sally's husband's uncle."

7.6   Relational graphs as implemented in this section cannot deal with general n-ary relations such as, "John gave the book to Mary." One could, however, represent the statement as a node with a VERB arc to GAVE, an AGENT arc to JOHN, an OBJECT arc to BOOK, and a DATIVE arc to MARY. Implement a question-answering system that uses such a data structure for a small domain.

Definitions of Some Useful Functions

A.1 REPEAT

(REPEAT "F1" "F2" . . . "Fn")

REPEAT (see Wise et al., (1975) is a FEXPR that allows one to write iterative LISP in a particularly convenient way. Each argument is either a form or a form preceded by the atom WHILE or by the atom UNTIL. At least one form of the series must be so preceded. These forms are evaluated in order, cyclicly until the form following an occurrence of WHILE evaluates to NIL or the form following an occurrence of UNTIL evaluates to non-NIL. REPEAT then returns the value of this last evaluated form. The premier example of the use of REPEAT is to write MEMBER:

(MEMBER S L)

If the S-expression S is a top level element of the list L, MEMBER returns T. Otherwise, it returns NIL.

```
(DEFPROP MEMBER
 (LAMBDA (S L)
  (REPEAT WHILE L
          UNTIL (EQUAL S (CAR L))
            (SETQ L (CDR L))))
 EXPR)
```

Other examples of the use of REPEAT are seen throughout this book.

```
(DEFPROP REPEAT
 (LAMBDA (BODI ALIST)
  (PROG   (REST VAL)
   TOP    (SETQ REST BODI)
   NEXT   (COND
```

```
            ((EQ (CAR REST) 'UNTIL)
             (COND
               ((SETQ VAL (EVAL (CADR REST) ALIST)) (RETURN VAL))
               (T (SETQ REST (CDR REST)))))
            ((EQ (CAR REST) 'WHILE)
             (COND ((EVAL (CADR REST) ALIST) (SETQ REST (CDR REST)))
                   (T (RETURN NIL))))
            (T (EVAL (CAR REST) ALIST)))
          (COND ((SETQ REST (CDR REST)) (GO NEXT)) (T (GO TOP)))))
FEXPR)
```

A.2 DATA, NTH, and MAKENTH

```
(DATA "TYPE" ("F1" "F2" . . . "Fn"))
```

DATA is a FEXPR designed to provide the LISP programmer with SNOBOL4-like programmer defined data types. After evaluation of (DATA TYPE (F1 F2 . . . Fn)), $n + 1$ new FEXPRs will be defined. Evaluation of

$$\text{(SETQ X (TYPE 'D1 . . . 'D}n\text{))}$$

will cause the value of X to be an expression of type TYPE with field Fi having value Di. (Fi X) will then evaluate to Di, and (SETQ X (Fi X 'G)) will change the value of the Fi field of X to G. The representation of an expression of type TYPE is a list whose first element is TYPE, and whose $(i + 1)$st element is the value of field Fi.

```
(DATA "TYPE" "LIST-OF-FIELDS")
```

Makes "TYPE" the name of a function for building the data type, and each field name in "LIST-OF-FIELDS" the name of a function for retrieving or changing the appropriate field.

```
(DEFPROP DATA
 (LAMBDA (TYFIELDS)
  (CONS (PUT (CAR TYFIELDS)
             'FEXPR
             (SUBST (CAR TYFIELDS)
                    'TP
                    '(LAMBDA (FLDS ALIST)
                      (CONS 'TP
                            (MAPCAR (FUNCTION
                                       (LAMBDA (X) (EVAL X ALIST)))
                                    FLDS)))))
        (DATADEF (CADR TYFIELDS) 2)))
FEXPR)
```

(DATADEF FIELDS N)

Makes the first atom of the list FIELDS the name of a function for retrieving or changing the Nth element of a list, and subsequent atoms the names of functions for subsequent elements.

```
(DEFPROP DATADEF
 (LAMBDA (FIELDS N)
  (COND   ((NULL FIELDS) NIL)
          (T (PUT (CAR FIELDS)
                  'FEXPR
                  (SUBST N
                         'N
                         '(LAMBDA (TNEW ALIST)
                             (COND ((CDR TNEW)
                                    (MAKENTH N
                                             (EVAL (CAR TNEW ALIST)
                                             (EVAL (CADR TNEW) ALIST)))
                                   (T (NTH N (EVAL (CAR TNEW) ALIST)))))))))
             (DATADEF (CDR FIELDS) (ADD1 N)))))
EXPR)
```

(NTH N L)

Returns the Nth top level member of the list L.

```
(DEFPROP NTH
 (LAMBDA (N L) (COND ((EQ N 1) (CAR L)) (T (NTH (SUB1 N) (CDR L)))))
EXPR)
```

(MAKENTH N L S)

Returns the list L with its Nth top level member changed to S.

```
(DEFPROP MAKENTH
 (LAMBDA (N L S)
  (COND   ((EQ N 1) (CONS S (CDR L)))
          (T (CONS (CAR L) (MAKENTH (SUB1 N) (CDR L) S)))))
EXPR)
```

A.3   PRIN3

(PRIN3 "FIELDS")

PRIN3 is a FEXPR that provides a formatted output facility. In the following list of fields, SEXP represents any LISP S-expression, NEXP represents an S-expression that evaluates to an integer, N represents an integer numeric atom, FIELD represents any PRIN3 fields except the last listed. Other characters represent themselves. Blanks are required where indicated.

SEXP	SEXP is printed unevaluated.
*SEXP	The value of SEXP is printed.
**SEXP	SEXP is evaluated, but not printed.
%NEXP	NEXP blanks are printed.
< >	A carriage return and line feed are printed.
;NEXP SEXP	NEXP instances of SEXP are printed unevaluated.
!NEXP L ! FIELD !	FIELD is printed in a field of NEXP positions, either
!NEXP C ! FIELD !	Left, Center, or Right justified.
!NEXP R ! FIELD !	

In the definitions below, we will assume that the following atoms already have values as indicated:

BLANK	An atom whose print name is one blank.
LPAR	An atom whose print name is a left parenthesis.
RPAR	An atom whose print name is a right parenthesis.

```
(DEFPROP PRIN3
 (LAMBDA (L ALIST)
  (REPEAT
   UNTIL (NULL L)
         (SETQ L (APPEND (PREF-OFF (CAR L)) (CDR L)))
         (COND
           ((EQ (CAR L) '*) (PRINC (EVAL (CADR L) ALIST))
                            (PRINC BLANK)
                            (SETQ L (CDDR L)))
           ((EQ (CAR L) '**) (EVAL (CADR L) ALIST)
                            (SETQ L (CDDR L)))
           ((EQ (CAR L) '%) (PRIN-N (EVAL (CADR L) ALIST) BLANK)
                            (SETQ L (CDDR L)))
           ((EQ (CAR L) '<>) (TERPRI) (SETQ L (CDR L)))
           ((EQ (CAR L) ';) (PRIN-N (EVAL (CADR L) ALIST) (CADDR L))
                            (PRINC BLANK)
                            (SETQ L (CDDDR L)))
           ((EQ (CAR L) '!) (SETQ L
                                  (SET-UP (EVAL (CADR L) ALIST)
                                          (CADDR L)
                                          (CDDDDR L)
                                          ALIST)))
           (T (PRINC (CAR L)) (PRINC BLANK) (SETQ L (CDR L)))))))
FEXPR)
```

(PREF-OFF A)

If A is an atom and its first character(s) are PRIN3 special characters, a list is returned whose CAR is an atom of the special characters and whose CADR is the rest of A. Otherwise, a list containing A unchanged is returned.

```
(DEFPROP PREF-OFF
 (LAMBDA (A) (PREF-OFF1 (EXPLODE A)))
EXPR)
(DEFPROP PREF-OFF1
 (LAMBDA (XA)
  (COND  ((NULL (CDR XA)) XA)
         ((EQUAL XA '(* *)) '(**))
         ((EQUAL XA '(< >)) '(<>))
         ((AND (CDDR XA) (EQ (CAR XA) '*) (EQ (CADR XA) '*))
          (LIST '** (READLIST (CDDR XA))))
         ((AND (CDDR XA) (EQ (CAR XA) '<) (EQ (CADR XA '>))
          (LIST '<> (READLIST (CDDR XA))))
         ((MEMBER (CAR XA) '(* % ; !))
          (CONS (CAR XA)
                (READLIST
                 (APPEND (LIST LPAR) (CDR XA) (LIST RPAR)))))
         (T (LIST (READLIST XA)))))
EXPR)
```

(PRIN-N N S)

Prints S N times without intervening blanks.

```
(DEFPROP PRIN-N
 (LAMBDA (N S)
  (REPEAT UNTIL (LESSP N 1) (PRINC S) (SETQ N (SUB1 N))))
EXPR)
```

(SET-UP WIDTH SIDE LST ALIST)

The beginning of the list LST, up to the first occurrence of the character ! are PRIN3 fields that are to be printed SIDE justified in a field of WIDTH positions. SET-UP rebuilds LST so that it represents the correct format without use of the character !. Any S-expressions that are evaluated are done so in the bindings of ALIST.

```
(DEFPROP SET-UP
 (LAMBDA (WIDTH SIDE LST ALIST)
  (PROG (LNGTH FRNT)
```

```
(SETQ LNGTH 0)
(REPEAT
 WHILE LST
        (SETQ LST (APPEND (PREF-OFF (CAR LST)) (CDR LST)))
  UNTIL (EQ (CAR LST) '!)
        (COND
          ((EQ (CAR LST) '*)
           (SETQ FRNT (CONS (LIST 'QUOTE
                                  (EVAL (CADR LST) ALIST))
                            (CONS '* FRNT)))
           (SETQ LNGTH (PLUS LNGTH (FLATSIZE (CADAR FRNT)) 1))
           (SETQ LST (CDDR LST)))
          ((EQ (CAR LST) '**) (EVAL (CADR LST) ALIST)
                              (SETQ LST (CDDR LST)))
          ((EQ (CAR LST) '%)
           (SETQ FRNT (CONS (EVAL (CADR LST) ALIST)
                            (CONS '% FRNT)))
           (SETQ LNGTH (PLUS LNGTH (CAR FRNT)))
           (SETQ LST (CDDR LST)))
          ((EQ (CAR LST) ';)
           (SETQ FRNT (CONS (CADDR LST)
                            (CONS (EVAL (CADR LST) ALIST)
                                  (CONS '; FRNT))))
           (SETQ LNGTH (PLUS LNGTH
                             (TIMES (CADR FRNT)
                                    (FLATSIZE (CAR FRNT)))
                             1))
           (SETQ LST (CDDDR LST)))
          (T (SETQ FRNT (CONS (CAR LST) FRNT))
             (SETQ LNGTH
                   (PLUS LNGTH (FLATSIZE (CAR FRNT)) 1))
             (SETQ LST (CDR LST)))))
(SETQ LNGTH (DIFFERENCE WIDTH LENGTH))
(SETQ LST
      (COND
        ((EQ SIDE 'L) (CONS '% (CONS LNGTH (CDR LST))))
        ((EQ SIDE 'C)
         (CONS '% (CONS (ROUND (QUOTIENT LNGTH 2.0))
                        (CDR LST))))
        (T (CDR LST))))
(REPEAT
 WHILE FRNT
        (SETQ LST (CONS (CAR FRNT) LST))
        (SETQ FRNT (CDR FRNT)))
```

```
      (SETQ LST
          (COND
            ((EQ SIDE 'C)
             (CONS '% (CONS (QUOTIENT LENGTH 2) LST)))
            ((EQ SIDE 'R) (CONS '% (CONS LNGTH LST)))
            (T LST)))
      (RETURN LST)))
EXPR)
```

(ROUND X)

Returns the integer closest to the real number X.

```
(DEFPROP ROUND
  (LAMBDA (X) (FIX (PLUS X 0.5)))
EXPR)
```

Appendix B
Functions
Assumed to be Predefined

B.1   LISP Functions Assumed to be Predefined

We list here the LISP functions that have been used but not defined in this book, because we have assumed them to be predefined in the LISP system in use. If your LISP does not have some of these or has some with slightly different definitions, it should not be too much trouble to either define them as presented here or change the definitions of the functions of the book as you implement them.

Arguments shown within quote marks are not evaluated before the function is evaluated. Otherwise, when we speak of an argument, we mean the value of the argument.

(ABS X)

The absolute value of the number X.

(ADD1 X)

$= X + 1$

(AND S1 S2 . . . Sn)

S1 . . . Sn are evaluated in order. As soon as one evaluates to NIL, NIL is returned. If none evaluates to NIL, T is returned.

(APPEND L1 L2 . . . Ln)

= a list consisting of all the top elements of L1 followed by all the top elements of L2 followed by . . . followed by all the top elements of Ln.

(ARRAY "ID" TYPE B1 B2 . . . Bn)

Declares an n dimensional array of type TYPE whose name is "ID". Each Bi should be of the form (LBi . UBi), meaning that dimension has lower bound LBi and upper bound UBi. In this book, the type is always T, meaning each element of the array is a LISP S-expression. An element of the array is referenced by the form ("ID" I1 I2 . . . In) where Ii is between LBi and UBi, inclusive. For setting the value of array elements, see STORE.

(ASCII N)

Creates and returns an atom whose single character print name has the ASCII code N. This atom is not INTERN'd, so multiple atoms with the same print name may result.

(ASSOC A LS)

Searches the list of S-expressions, LS, for an S-expression whose CAR is EQ to A. The first one found is returned. If none is found, NIL is returned.

(ATOM S)

= T if S is an atom, NIL otherwise.

(CAR S)

If S is a list, returns the first top level element of S. If S is a dotted pair, returns the first element of the pair. (Both these statements say the same thing.)

(CDR S)

If S is a list, returns S with its CAR deleted. If S is a dotted pair, returns the second element of the pair. (Both these statements say the same thing.)

(CAAR S)

= (CAR (CAR S))

(CAADR S)

= (CAR (CAR (CDR S)))

(CADAR S)

= (CAR (CDR (CAR S)))

(CADADR S)

= (CAR (CDR (CAR (CDR S))))

(CADR S)

= (CAR (CDR S))

(CADDR S)

= (CAR (CDR (CDR S)))

(CADDDR S)

$$= (CAR (CDR (CDR (CDR S))))$$

(CDAR S)

$$= (CDR(CAR S))$$

(CDADR S)

$$= (CDR (CAR (CDR S)))$$

(CDDR S)

$$= (CDR (CDR S))$$

(CDDDR S)

$$= (CDR (CDR (CDR S)))$$

(CDDDDR S)

$$= (CDR (CDR (CDR (CDR S))))$$

(COND $(S1, 1 \ S1, 2 \ldots S1, k1)$
$(S2, 1 \ S2, 2 \ldots S2, k2)$

.

.

.

$(Sn, 1 \ Sn, 2 \ldots Sn, kn))$
where n is equal to or greater than 1, and each ki is equal to or greater than 1.
Evaluates the $Si,1$ in order until one of them, $Sj,1$ say, evaluates to anything
other than NIL.   Then $Sj,2$ through Sj,kj are evaluated in order and the
value of Sj,kj is returned.   If all the $Si,1$ evaluate to NIL, NIL is returned.

(CONS S1 S2)

If S2 is a list, a list is returned whose **CAR** is S1 and whose subsequent
elements are the elements of S2.   Otherwise, the dotted pair (S1 . S2) is returned. (Both these statements say the same thing.)

(DEFPROP "ID" "V" "P")

V is put as the value of the property P on the property list of the atom ID.
ID is returned.
The main use of **DEFPROP** in this book is to define functions, since in the
LISP used by the author, a function is defined by putting the lambda ex-
pression which is to be the definition on the property list of the atom which
is to be the function's name as the value of the property EXPR or FEXPR.

(DIFFERENCE X1 X2 . . . Xn)

$$= X1 - X2 - . . , - Xn$$

(EQ X Y)

Returns T if X and Y are the same atoms or numbers. Otherwise, returns NIL.

(EQUAL X Y)

Returns T if X and Y are equivalent S-expressions. Otherwise, returns NIL.

(ERRSET "S" "F")

Evaluates S, and if no error occurs during the evaluation, returns a list whose sole element is the value of S. If an error does occur during the evaluation, and F is not NIL, then no error message is printed and NIL is returned. This is used in this book to read an auxiliary file and "trap" the end-of-file error message.

(EVAL S ALIST)

Evaluates S and returns its value.
The second argument may be omitted. If so, S is evaluated in the "current" environment. If ALIST is present, it must be an "association list" of variables and values, and S is evaluated in that environment. Such an "association list" is created by the system when a FEXPR that has a second lambda variable is evaluated.

(EVALQUOTE FN L)

The function FN is evaluated with the elements of the list L as its arguments.

(EVLIS L)

Returns a list of the values of the elements of the list L.

(EXPLODE S)

Returns a list of single character atoms which would be the characters printed by (PRINC S).

(FIX X)

The largest integer not greater than X.

(FLATSIZE S)

Returns the number of characters required to print S.
= (LENGTH (EXPLODE S))

(FLOAT X)

The floating point number equal to X.

(FUNCTION "FN")

Like (QUOTE "FN"), but preferable when FN is a lambda expression or function name for reasons we will not discuss.

(GE X Y)

> T if X is greater than or equal to Y, NIL otherwise.

(GENSYM)

> Returns a newly created atom which is different from any other atom. The print name of the atom is of the form Gnnnn, where nnnn is an integer.

(GET A P)

> Returns the value of the property P on the property list of the atom A. If there is no property P on A's property list, NIL is returned. Note the confusion if P is on A's property list but its value is NIL.

(GO "LABEL")

> Used within a PROG to transfer control to the label LABEL. The only use of GO in this book is in Appendix A.1 in the definition of REPEAT.

(GREATERP X1 X2 . . . Xn)

> T if $X1 > X2 > \ldots > Xn$

(INC CHAN ACTION)

> Selects the channel whose name is CHAN for input. That is, future input will be from that channel. Returns the name of the previously selected channel, which is closed if ACTION is T, but only deselected if ACTION is NIL. The name of the standard channel (the interactive terminal) is NIL.

(INPUT "DEVICE" "FILE")

> Establishes a channel to read from the file FILE, which is on the device DEVICE (in our use of INPUT, the device is always the disk, DSK:). INPUT returns T as the name of the new channel.

(INSERT S L)

> If S is EQUAL to some top level element of the list L, L is returned. Otherwise (CONS S L) is returned.

(INTERN A)

> Searches the system's "list" of atoms for one with the same print name as the atom A. If one is found, it is returned. Otherwise A is put on that "list" and returned.

(LE X Y)

> T if X is less than or equal to Y

(LENGTH L)

> Returns the number of top level elements on the list L.

(LESSP X1 X2 . . . X*n*)

> T if $X1 < X2 < \ldots < Xn$

(LIST S1 S2 . . . S*n*)

> The list whose top level elements are $S1, S2, \ldots, Sn$.

(MAPC FN L)

> FN must be a function of one argument and L must be a list. MAPC applies FN to each top level element of L in succession and returns NIL.

(MAPCAR FN L)

> FN must be a function of one argument and L must be a list. MAPC applies FN to each top level element of L in succession and returns a list of the values in order.

(MAX X Y)

> if $X > Y$, then X, otherwise Y

(MEMBER S L)

> Returns T if the S-expression S is EQUAL to any top level element of the list L, and returns NIL otherwise.

(MIN X Y)

> if $X < Y$, then X, otherwise Y

(MINUS X)

> $= -X$

(MINUSP X)

> T if X is a negative number, NIL if X is a nonnegative number

(NOT S)

> Returns T if S is NIL, otherwise returns NIL.

(NULL S)

> Returns T if S is NIL, otherwise returns NIL.

(NUMBERP X)

> T if X is a number, NIL otherwise

(OR "S1" "S2" . . . "S*n*")

> Evaluates the Si in order until one of them evaluates to non-NIL. It then returns that value. If all the Si evaluate to NIL, NIL is returned.

(PLUS X1 X2 . . . X*n*)

$$= X1 + X2 + \ldots + Xn$$

(PRINC S)

Prints the S-expression S on the selected output channel with no preceding or following blanks.

(PRINT S)

Prints the S-expression S on the selected output channel, preceded by a carriage return — line feed and followed by a blank.

(PROG "VARLIST" "FORM1" "FORM2" . . . "FORM*n*")

VARLIST is a list of atoms which are bound as local variables and given the initial value of NIL. The FORM*i* are evaluated in order and NIL is returned. However, if the function RETURN is evaluated within the PROG, the PROG is exited returning the value returned by RETURN.

(PROG2 "FORM1" "FORM2" . . . "FORM*n*")

The FORM*i* are evaluated in order and the value of FORM2 is returned. *n* must be equal to or greater than 2.

(PUT A P V)

V is put as the value of the property P on the property list of the atom A.

(QUOTE "S")

"S" is returned unevaluated. In this book, we use 'S to abbreviate (QUOTE S).

(QUOTIENT X1 X2 . . . X*n*)

$$= X1 \,/\, X2 \,/\, \ldots \,/\, Xn$$

(RAC L)

Returns the last top level element of the list L.

(RDC L)

Returns a copy of the list L with the last top level element deleted.

(READ)

Reads and returns the next S-expression from the selected input channel.

(READLIST LAT)

LAT is a list of atoms with single character print names. READLIST returns the S-expression that READ would return if those characters appeared next in the selected input channel.

(REMAINDER X Y)

$$= X - (X / Y) * Y$$
X and Y must be integers.

(REMOVE S L)

Returns the list L with the first top level occurrence of the S-expression S removed.

(RETURN S)

Returns S and causes the PROG containing the RETURN to return with the same value. S may be omitted, in which case NIL is returned.

(REVERSE L)

Returns a copy of the list L with the top level elements in the reverse order.

(SASSOC A LS FN)

Searches the list of S-expressions, LS, for an S-expression whose CAR is EQ to A. The first one found is returned. If none is found, the value of FN, a function of no arguments, is returned.

(SET A S)

The value of the atom A is changed to S. S is returned.

(SETQ "A" S)

$$= (SET (QUOTE \text{ "A"}) S)$$

(SNOC L S)

Returns a list whose last element is S and whose previous elements are the elements of the list L.

(SPRINT S N 1)

Prints the S-expression S in a "pretty" format starting in column N.

(STORE ("ID" I1 I2 . . . In) VALUE)

Changes the value of the specified array element to VALUE, and returns VALUE. (see ARRAY)

(SUBST NEW OLD S)

Returns a copy of the S-expression S with all S-expressions EQUAL to OLD replaced by the S-expression NEW.

(SUB1 X)

$$= X - 1$$

(TERPRI S)

> Prints a carriage return and line feed and returns S. S may be omitted, in which case NIL is returned.

(TIME)

> Returns the number of milliseconds of compute time used by the job since logging into the system.

(TIMES X1 X2 ... X*n*)

> = X1 * X2 * ... * X*n*

(TYI)

> Reads the next character from the selected input channel and returns the ASCII code for that character.

(ZEROP N)

> Returns T if N is zero. Returns NIL if it is any other number.

B.2 MICROPLANNER Functions Assumed to be Predefined

(THASSERT "ASSERTION" "RECOMMENDATION")

> If the ASSERTION is not already in the data base, it is added in, and any THANTEcedent theorems recommended by the RECOMMENDATION whose patterns match ASSERTION are invoked. If the ASSERTION is already in the data base, the THASSERT fails, causing backup. If the THASSERT is backed into, the ASSERTION is removed from the data base and backup continues.

(THERASE "ASSERTION" "RECOMMENDATION")

> If the ASSERTION is in the data base, it is removed, and any THERASING theorems recommended by the RECOMMENDATION whose patterns match the ASSERTION are invoked. If the ASSERTATION is not in the data base, the THERASE fails, causing backup. If the THERASE is backed into, the ASSERTION is replaced into the data base and backup continues.

(THGOAL "ASSERTION" "RECOMMENDATION")

> If the ASSERTION is found in the data base, THGOAL succeeds. If it is not found, THCONSEquent theorems recommended by the RECOMMENDATION whose patterns match the ASSERTION are invoked one at a time until one succeeds or they all fail. If one succeeds, the THGOAL succeeds. If they all fail, the THGOAL fails causing backup. If the THGOAL is backed into, it tries to succeed in a different way than the last time(s). If this fails, backup continues. Otherwise, control goes forward again.

B.3   SNOBOL4 Functions Assumed to be Predefined

When an argument is shown in quotes, it indicates that the corresponding argument must be a string satisfying the syntax indicated.

CONVERT(OBJECT, 'DATATYPE')

Returns an object of type DATATYPE which is the conversion of the object OBJECT of whatever type it is. Fails if the conversion is undefined (see Sec. 7.2.1 of Griswold et al., 1971).

DATA('TYPE(FIELD1, . . . , FIELDn)')

Defines a datatype of type TYPE whose fields are named FIELD1,...,FIELDn. Defines a TYPE valued function named TYPE whose arguments are the values of the fields of a new object of that type. Defines n functions named FIELD1, ..., FIELDn which are functions of one object of type TYPE and can be used either for accessing the values of the fields of the object or for storing into the fields.

DEFINE('FUNCTION(ARG1, . . . , ARGn) VAR1, . . . , VARk')

Defines a function named FUNCTION with formal arguments ARG1,..., ARGn and local variables VAR1,..., VARk whose body starts at the statement labeled FUNCTION.

DIFFER(X, Y)

Fails if X and Y are identical objects. Succeeds otherwise. If Y is omitted, X will be compared with the null string.

GT(X, Y)

Succeeds if the number X is greater than the number Y. Fails otherwise.

IDENT(X, Y)

Succeeds if X and Y are identical objects. Fails otherwise. If Y is omitted, X will be compared with the null string.

LEN(N)

Returns a pattern that matches any string of length N.

LT(X, Y)

Succeeds if the number X is less than the number Y.

PROTOTYPE(ARRAY)

Returns the prototype of the array ARRAY. If ARRAY has k dimensions, the prototype will be a string of the form '$lb_1 : ub_1 ,..., lb_k : ub_k$' where lb_i and ub_i are, respectively, the lower and upper bounds of the ith dimension of ARRAY.

TAB(N)

Returns a pattern that matches the substring beginning at the current cursor position and ending at the Nth character from the left end of the subject string.

TABLE( )

Returns a new object of type table.

Index to
Definitions of Functions

Each function used in the book is listed followed by an entry of the form
p: $s1, \ldots, sk$ meaning that the function is defined on page p and used in sections $s1, \ldots, sk$.
In a few cases, several functions have been defined and used in different sections with
the same name. In those cases, the entry is of the form $p1$: $s11, \ldots s1k1; \ldots;$
pn: $sn1, \ldots, snkn$ meaning that in section sij, the definition on page pi is in force.

ABS, 148: 5.2
ABTAN, 93: 5.2
ACTION, 126: 7
ADD, 128: 7
ADDL, 60: 4.1
ADDNEW, 77: 4.2
ADDR, 61: 4.1
ADD1, 148: 1.1, 3.2, 4.2, 5.2, 6, A.2
ADD . VOTES, 80: 5.1
ADD-TO-OPEN, 2: 1.1
ALTMOVE, 48: 3.2
AND, 148: 2.2, 3.2, 4.1, 4.2, 7, A.3
AND?, 65: 4.2
AND-NODE, 11: 1.2
APPEND, 148: 1.1, 1.2, 3.2, 4.2, 5.2, 7, A.3
APPLY-RULE, 126: 7
APPLY-RULE-1, 128: 7
APPLY-SUBST, 76: 4.2
APPLY-TESTS, 127: 7
ARRAY, 148: 5.2
ASCII, 149: 5.2
ASSOC, 149: 4.2
ASSOCIATE, 17: 1.2
ASSOCIATE 1, 18: 1.2
ATOM, 149: 4.1, 4.2, 7
AVSO, 10: 1.2
BACKUP, 15: 1.2
BETTER, 4: 1.1
BICOND?, 66: 4.2
BUILD, 14: 1.2

BUMP, 61: 4.1
CAPMOVE, 46: 3.2
CAPMOVE 1, 46: 3.2
CAR, 149: 1.1, 1.2, 2.1, 2.2, 3.1, 3.2, 4.1,
    4.2, 5.2, 6, 7, A.1, A.2, A.3
CDR, 149: 1.1, 1.2, 3.1, 3.2, 4.1, 4.2, 5.2,
    6, 7, A.1, A.2, A.3
CAAR, 149: 1.2, 4.2, 5.2
CAADR, 149: 1.2, 5.2
CADAR, 149: 1.2, A.3
CADADR, 149: 1.2
CADR, 149: 1.1, 1.2, 2.2, 3.2, 4.1, 4.2, 5.2,
    7, A.1, A.2, A.3
CADDR, 149: 1.1, 3.2, 4.1, 4.2, 5.2, 7, A.3
CADDDR, 150: 7
CDAR, 150: 4.2, 5.2
CDADR, 150: 5.2
CDDR, 150: 1.1, 4.2, 5.2, 7, A.3
CDDDR, 150: A.3
CDDDDR, 150: A.3
CHANGEVAL, 38: 3.2
CHECKCAP, 41: 3.2
CHECKMT, 41: 3.2
CHOOSE, 51: 3.2
CLASS, 80: 5.1
CLAUSE, 63: 4.2
CLAUSES, 66: 4.2
CLAUSEFORM, 66: 4.2
CLAUSE-IT, 67: 4.2
CNF, 70: 4.2

CNF1, 70: 4.2
COMPLEMENT, 130: 7
COMPOSE1, 77: 4.2
COMPOSE-SUBST, 76: 4.2
CONCAVE?, 95: 5.2
COND, 150: 1.1, 1.2, 2.2, 3.1, 3.2, 4.1, 4.2,
    5.2, 6, 7, A.1, A.2, A.3
COND?, 65: 4.2
CONDELIM, 67: 4.2
CONDELIM1, 67: 4.2
CONS, 150: 1.1, 1.2, 3.2, 4.2, 5.2, 6, 7,
    A.2, A.3
CONVERT, 157: 5.1
CROSS, 26: 2.2
CUE, 111: 6
CUE-LIST, 110: 6
CUTOFF, 34: 3.1
C-SEARCH, 91: 5.2
DATA, 142: 1.1, 1.2, 4.1, 4.2, 6; 157: 5.1
DATADEF, 143: A.2
DEAD, 35: 3.1; 44: 3.2
DEFINE, 157: 5.1
DEFPROP, 150: 1.1, 1.2, 2.1, 2.2, 3.1, 3.2,
    4.1, 4.2, 5.2, 6, 7, A.1, A.2, A.3
DETECTOR, 79: 5.1
DIFFER, 157: 5.1
DIFFERENCE, 150: 2.1, 3.2, 5.2, 6, A.3
DISCRIMINATE, 113: 6
DISJOINT, 59: 4.1
DISPLAY, 112: 6
DISTRIB, 16: 1.2; 70: 4.2
DISTRIB1, 16: 1.2
DISTRIB2, 17: 1.2
DISTRIB&, 15: 1.2
DNF, 15: 1.2
DROP, 42: 3.2
DSLOPE, 88: 5.2
D-LEARN, 114: 6
EMPTY, 38: 3.2
END, 34: 3.1; 43: 3.2
ENDGAME, 49: 3.2
END1, 88: 5.2
END2, 88: 5.2
EPAM, 111: 6
EQ, 151: 1.1, 1.2, 2.2, 3.2, 4.1, 4.2, 5.2, 6,
    7, A.1, A.2, A.3
EQPNODE, 19: 1.2
EQSETS, 19: 1.2
EQUAL, 151: 1.1, 1.2, 4.2, 5.2, 6, A.3
EQUIV, 136: 7
EQUIV1, 136: 7
EQUIV-COMPRESS, 135: 7
EQUIV-COMP1, 135: 7
ERRSET, 151: 5.2
EVAL, 151: 5.2, 6, 7, A.1, A.2, A.3
EVALQUOTE, 151: 4.1, 7
EVLIS, 151: 7
EXPAND, 3: 1.1; 11: 1.2; 35: 3.1; 45: 3.2
EXPAND1, 13: 1.2; 45: 3.2

EXPAND2, 13: 1.2
EXPLODE, 151: 3.2, A.3
EXTEND, 96: 5.2; 130: 7
EXTENDM, 129: 7
EXTEND-CONCAVE, 95: 5.2
FALSE, 109: 6
FHAT, 2: 1.1
FIND-CONTOUR, 90: 5.2
FIND-CUE, 116: 6
FIND-PART, 115: 6
FIND-TEST, 116: 6
FIRST-OR, 16: 1.2
FIX, 151: A.3
FLATSIZE, 151: A.3
FLOAT, 151: 5.2
FOLLOW, 96: 5.2
FOLLOW1, 98: 5.2
FOLLOW2, 98: 5.2
FOLLOW-C, 97: 5.2
FOLLOW-R, 96: 5.2
FOLLOW-S, 98: 5.2
FOLLOW-S1, 99: 5.2
FUNCTION, 151: 1.1, 1.2, 3.2, 4.1, 4.2, 5.2,
    6, 7, A.2
GE, 152: 3.1
GENERIC, 131: 7
GENERIC-GENERIC, 132: 7
GENSYM, 152: 4.2, 7
GET, 152: 1.1, 3.2, 4.2, 6, 7
GETMOVE, 49: 3.2
GET&NODES, 13: 1.2
GET-SENTENCE, 124: 7
GHAT, 2: 1.1, 1.2
GO, 152: A.1
GOAL?, 6: 1.1; 11: 1.2
GREATERP, 152: 2.2, 3.2, 5.2, 6
GT, 157: 5.1
HHAT, 6: 1.1; 20: 1.2
IDENT, 157: 5.1
IMAGE, 110: 6
IMAGE-LIST, 110: 6
IMPLICATION, 80: 5.1
IMPLIED, 79, 80: 5.1
INC, 152: 5.2
INITBRD, 47: 3.2
INITIALIZE, 126: 7
INPUT, 152: 5.2
INSERT, 152: 4.1, 4.2
INSERTO, 5: 1.1
INSERTPN, 18: 1.2
INTERN, 152: 5.2
KALAH, 47: 3.2
KALAHR, 37: 3.2
LA, 58: 4.1
LCLAUSE, 63: 4.2
LDIAG, 24: 2.1
LE, 152: 3.1, 3.2
LEARN, 83: 5.1; 113: 6
LEN, 157: 5.1

LENGTH, 152: 1.2, 5.2
LESSP, 153: 1.1, 1.2, 3.2, 5.2, A.3
LE*, 27: 2.2
LF, 58: 4.1
LINE, 58: 4.1; 63: 4.2; 92: 5.2
LINES, 92: 5.2
LIST, 153: 1.1, 1.2, 2.1, 2.2, 3.2, 4.2, 5.2,
    7, A.3
LIST-CLS, 64: 4.2
LIST-SOLN, 5: 1.1
LOC-CORNER, 90: 5.2
LT, 157: 5.1
LVL, 58: 4.1
MAKE, 3: 1.1; 12: 1.2; 51: 3.2
MAKENTH, 143: 6, A.2
MAKETNODE, 14: 1.2
MAKE&NODE, 14: 1.2
MAKE*, 12: 1.2
MAKE-TEST-NODE, 115: 6
MAPC, 153: 1.1, 3.2, 5.2, 7
MAPCAR, 153: 1.2, 4.2, 6, A.2
MARK-ENDS, 89: 5.2
MARK-LINE, 89: 5.2
MATCH, 126: 7
MATCH1, 127: 7
MAX, 153: 3.1, 5.2
MAXER, 34: 3.1; 44: 3.2
MEFIRST?, 48: 3.2
MEMBER, 153: 4.1, 4.2, 5.2, 7, A.3
MERGE, 74: 4.2
MERGE1, 74: 4.2
MIN, 153: 3.1
MINISCOPE, 68: 4.2
MINISCOPE1, 68: 4.2
MINUS, 153: 2.2, 3.2
MINUSP, 153: 5.2
MIN-STAT, 17: 1.2
MOVE, 27: 2.2; 40: 3.2
MOVEOF, 43: 3.2
MOVE1, 40: 3.2
MTSIDE, 42: 3.2
MTSIDEP, 41: 3.2
MULT, 43: 3.2
MULTMOVE, 45: 3.2
M-T-N-1, 115: 6
M-T-N-2, 115: 6
NEGATE, 68: 4.2
NEGATE1, 68: 4.2
NEG?, 65: 4.2
NEWVAR, 69: 4.2
NEXT, 79: 5.1
NIL-ON, 72: 4.2
NODE, 2: 1.1, 1.2
NOT, 153: 1.2, 2.2, 3.2, 4.1, 4.2, 5.2, 6, 7
NTH, 143: 5.2, 6, A.2
NULL, 153: 1.1, 1.2, 3.1, 3.2, 4.1, 4.2, 5.2,
    6, 7, A.2, A.3
NUM, 37: 3.2
NUMBERP, 153: 3.2

OCCUR-IN, 76: 4.2
OMOVE, 49: 3.2
ON?, 4: 1.1
OP, 64: 4.2
OPP, 39: 3.2
OR, 153: 1.2, 2.2, 3.2, 4.2, 6
OR-NODE, 11: 1.2
OR?, 65: 4.2
OTHER, 27: 2.2; 36: 3.2
OWNER, 36: 3.2
OWNR, 136: 7
OWNRGU, 137: 7
OWNRGUQ, 137: 7
OWNRQ, 136: 7
OWNRSGQ, 137: 7
PARENT, 2: 1.1
PART, 109: 6
PATH, 128: 7
PATHR, 38: 3.2
PATH1, 129: 7
PATNO, 81: 5.1
PATTERN, 79: 5.1; 125: 7
PLACE, 24: 2.1
PLAY, 50: 3.2
PLAYER, 43: 3.2
PLAY1, 50: 3.2
PLUS, 154: 1.1, 1.2, 2.1, 2.2, 3.2, 4.1, 5.2,
    6, A.3
PMOVE, 50: 3.2
PNODE, 10: 1.2
POINT, 87: 5.2
POINT?, 87: 5.2
POPVAL, 38: 3.2
POTR, 36: 3.2
PREF-OFF, 145: A.3
PREF-OFF1, 145: A.3
PRIMITIVE, 20: 1.2
PRIM-NO, 58: 4.1
PRIM-YES, 59: 4.1
PRINC, 154: A.3
PRINLINE, 61: 4.1
PRINT, 154: 1.1
PRINTBRD, 47: 3.2
PRIN3, 143: 2.1, 2.2, 3.2, 4.1, 4.2, 5.2, 6, 7
PRIN-N, 145: A.3
PRIN-VIEW, 86: 5.2
PRLST, 61: 4.1
PROCESS, 124: 7
PROCESS-1, 124: 7
PROG, 154: 1.1, 1.2, 3.2, 4.1, 4.2, 5.2, 6, 7,
    A.1, A.3
PROG2, 154: 3.1, 3.2, 4.1, 4.2, 6, 7
PROTOTYPE, 157: 5.1
PROVE, 58: 4.1; 63: 4.2
PUSHVAL, 37: 3.2
PUT, 154: 1.1, 3.2, 4.2, 6, 7, A.2
QUANTIFIER?, 66: 4.2
QUOTE, 154: 1.1, 1.2, 2.2, 3.2, 4.1, 4.2, 5.2,
    6, 7, A.1, A.2, A.3

QUOTIENT, 154: 5.2, 6, A.3
RA, 58: 4.1
RAC, 154: 5.2, 7
RANDOM, 110: 6
RDC, 154: 5.2
RDIAG, 24: 2.1
READ, 154: 3.2, 6, 7
READLIST, 154: 3.2, A.3
RECOGNIZE, 80: 5.1
REDL, 59: 4.1
REDR, 60: 4.1
REMAINDER, 155: 6
REMOVE, 155: 1.1, 1.2
REMOVE*, 74: 4.2
RENAME, 71: 4.2
REPEAT, 141: 1.1, 1.2, 3.2, 5.2, 6, 7, A.3
REPORT, 28: 2.2; 51: 3.2
RESOLVE, 71: 4.2
RESPOND, 112: 6
RESPOND1, 112: 6
RETURN, 155: 1.1, 1.2, 3.2, 5.2, 7, A.1, A.3
REVERSE, 155: 3.2, 5.2, 7
RF, 58: 4.1
RMAPCAR, 128: 7
ROTATE, 19: 1.2
ROUND, 147: A.3
SAFE, 27: 2.2
SASSOC, 155: 4.2, 6
SEARCH, 1: 1.1; 32: 3.1
SEARCH1, 32: 3.1
SEARCH2, 33: 3.1
SET, 155: 6, 7
SETPATH, 39: 3.2
SETQ, 155: 1.1, 1.2, 2.2, 3.1, 3.2, 4.1, 4.2,
      5.2, 6, 7, A.1, A.3
SETR, 133: 7
SETRQ, 133: 7
SETRS, 134: 7
SETRSQ, 134: 7
SETRS1, 134: 7
SETRS1Q, 135: 7
SETSYM, 39: 3.2
SET-UP, 145: A.3
SET-VIEW, 87: 5.2
SIDER, 39: 3.2
SIGN, 97: 5.2
SIR, 123: 7
SKOLEMIZE, 69: 4.2
SKOLEM1, 69: 4.2
SLOPE, 88: 5.2
SNOC, 155: 1.1, 4.2, 7
SPECIFIC, 131: 7
SPECIFIC-GENERIC, 132: 7
SPECIFY, 134: 7
SPECIFY1, 135: 7
SPLIT, 132: 7
SPLIT1, 132: 7

SPRINT, 155: 6
STANDARDIZE, 68: 4.2
STANDARDIZE1, 69: 4.2
START, 34: 3.1; 43: 3.2
START-IMAGE, 114: 6
STATE, 2: 1.1; 10: 1.2
STATIC, 35: 3.1; 44: 3.2
STATUS, 10: 1.2
STORE, 155: 5.2
STORE-CUE, 117: 6
STORE-VIEW, 85: 5.2
STRAIGHT-C, 97: 5.2
STRAIGHT-R, 97: 5.2
SUBST, 155: 4.2, A.2
SUB1, 155: 2.1, 3.1, 3.2, 5.2, A.2, A.3
SUCCESSORS, 10: 1.2
TAB, 158: 5.1
TABLE, 158: 5.1
TAKE, 42: 3.2
TAN, 93: 5.2
TERMINAL?, 15: 1.2
TERPRI, 156: A.3
TEST, 109: 6
TESTS, 125: 7
TEST-NODE, 109: 6
TEST?, 110: 6
THASSERT, 156: 2.1, 2.2
THERASE, 156: 2.1, 2.2
THGOAL, 156: 2.1, 2.2
TIME, 156: 3.2
TIMES, 156: 3.2, 5.2, 6, A.3
TREE, 111: 6
TRIP-SEG, 6: 1.1
TRUE, 109: 6
TRY-CLASH, 73: 4.2
TRY-CLASHES, 72: 4.2
TRY-CLASH1, 73: 4.2
TRY-SLOPES, 99: 5.2
TYI, 156: 5.2
UNIFY, 74: 4.2
UNIFY1, 75: 4.2
UNIFY2, 75: 4.2
UNION, 130: 7
UNIONPN, 18: 1.2
UNIQUE, 131: 7
UNIQUE-GENERIC, 132: 7
UNMARK-ENDS, 96: 5.2
UPDATE, 84: 5.1
VALUE, 37: 3.2
VARIABLES, 125: 7
VARIABLE?, 72: 4.2
VBLS, 72: 4.2
VIEW-IN, 86: 5.2
WANG, 58: 4.1
WEIGHT, 79, 80: 5.1
WINNER, 81: 5.1
ZEROP, 156: 2.2, 3.2, 5.2

Bibliography

Allen, J. (1978). *The Anatomy of LISP.* New York: McGraw-Hill.

Banerji, R. B. (1969). *Theory of Problem Solving: An Approach to Artificial Intelligence.* New York: American Elsevier.

Baumgart, B. G. (1972). Micro-planner alternate reference manual. SAILON No. 67. Stanford: Stanford Artificial Intelligence Laboratory.

Berkeley, E. C., and Bobrow, D. G., eds. (1964). *The Programming Language LISP: Its Operation and Applications.* Cambridge, Mass.: Information International.

Chang, C. L., and Lee, R. C. T. (1973). *Symbolic Logic and Mechanical Theorem Proving.* New York: Academic Press.

Chang, C. L., and Slagle, J. R. (1971). An admissable and optimal algorithm for searching AND/OR graphs. *Artificial Intelligence, 2:* 117-128.

Feigenbaum, E. A. (1963). The simulation of verbal learning behavior. In: *Computers and Thought* (Feigenbaum, E. A., and Feldman, J., eds.). New York: McGraw-Hill, pp. 297-309.

Feigenbaum, E. A., and Feldman, J., eds. (1963). *Computers and Thought.* New York: McGraw-Hill.

Friedman, D. P. (1974). *The Little LISPer.* Palo Alto: Science Research Associates.

Gimpel, J. F. (1976). *Algorithms in SNOBOL4.* New York: Wiley.

Griswold, R. E. (1972). *The Macro Implementation of SNOBOL4.* San Francisco: Freeman.

Griswold, R. E. (1975). *String and List Processing in SNOBOL4: Techniques and Applications.* Englewood Cliffs, N. J.: Prentice-Hall.

Griswold, R. E., and Griswold, M. T. (1973). *A SNOBOL4 Primer.* Englewood Cliffs, N. J.: Prentice-Hall.

Griswold, R. E., Poage, J. F., and Polonsky, I. P. (1971). *The SNOBOL4 Programming Language Second Edition.* Englewood Cliffs, N. J.: Prentice-Hall.

Gyllenskog, J. H. (1976). Konane as a vehicle for teaching AI. *SIGART Newsletter,* No. 56: 5-6.

Hart, P., Nilsson, N., and Raphael, B. (1968). A formal basis for the heuristic determination of minimum cost paths. *IEEE Trans. Sys. Sci. and Cybernetics*, SSC-4, no. 2: 100-107.

Hunt, E. B. (1975). *Artificial Intelligence.* New York: Academic Press.

Jackson, P. C. (1974). *Introduction to Artificial Intelligence.* New York: Petrocelli/ Charter.

Knuth, D. E. (1969). *The Art of Computer Programming: Volume 2/Seminumerical Algorithms.* Reading, Mass.: Addison-Wesley.

McCarthy, J., Abrahams, P. W., Edwards, D. J., Hart, T. P., and Levin, M. I. (1963). *LISP 1.5 Programmer's Manual.* Cambridge, Mass.: MIT Press.

Maurer, W. D. (1973). *A Programmer's Introduction to LISP.* New York: American Elsevier.

Maurer, W. D. (1976). *The Programmer's Introduction to SNOBOL.* New York: American Elsevier.

Newborn, M. (1975). *Computer Chess.* New York: Academic Press.

Nilsson, N. (1971). *Problem-Solving Methods in Artificial Intelligence.* New York: McGraw-Hill.

Raphael, B. (1964). A computer program which 'understands'. *Proceedings of the Fall Joint Computer Conference.* Montvale, N. J.: AFIPS Press, pp. 577-589.

Raphael, B. (1968). SIR: semantic information retrieval. In: *Semantic Information Processing* (M. Minsky, ed.). Cambridge, Mass.: MIT Press, pp. 33-145.

Raphael, B. (1976). *The Thinking Computer: Mind Inside Matter.* San Francisco: Freeman.

Robinson, J. A. (1965). A machine-oriented logic based on the resolution principle. *Journal of the ACM*, 12: 23-41.

Shirai, Y. (1975). Analyzing intensity arrays using knowledge about scenes. In: *The Psychology of Computer Vision* (Winston, P. H., ed.). New York: McGraw-Hill, pp. 93-113.

Siklóssy, L. S. (1976). *Let's Talk LISP.* Englewood Cliffs, N. J.: Prentice-Hall.

Slagle, J. R. (1971). *Artificial Intelligence: The Heuristic Programming Approach.* New York: McGraw-Hill.

Sussman, G. J., and Winograd, T. (1970). Micro-planner reference manual. AI Memo 203. Cambridge, Mass.: M. I. T. Artificial Intelligence Laboratory.

Uhr, L. (1973). *Pattern Recognition, Learning, and Thought.* Englewood Cliffs, N. J.: Prentice-Hall.

Wang, H. (1960). Toward mechanical mathematics. *IBM Journal of Research and Development,* 4: 2-22. Reprinted in *The Modeling of Mind: Computers and Intelligence* (Sayre, K. M., and Crosson, F. J., eds.). New York: Simon and Schuster, 1963.

Weisman, C. (1968). *LISP 1.5 Primer.* Belmont, Calif.: Dickenson.

Winston, P. H., ed. (1975a). *The Psychology of Computer Vision.* New York: McGraw-Hill.

Winston, P. H. (1975b). Learning structural descriptions from examples. Ibid, pp. 157-209.

Winston, P. H. (1977). *Artificial Intelligence.* Reading, Mass.: Addison-Wesley.

Wirth, N. (1971). Program development by stepwise refinement. *Communications of the ACM,* 14: 221-227.

Wise, D., Friedman, D. P., Shapiro, S. C., and Wand, M. (1975). Boolean-valued loops. *BIT,* 15: 431-451.